SERIES

A life-changing encounter
with God's Word from the book of

DANIEL

NAVPRESS

*A NavPress published resource in alliance
with Tyndale House Publishers, Inc.*

D0006596

NavPress is the publishing ministry of The Navigators, an international Christian organization and leader in personal spiritual development. NavPress is committed to helping people grow spiritually and enjoy lives of meaning and hope through personal and group resources that are biblically rooted, culturally relevant, and highly practical.

For a free catalog go to www.NavPress.com.

ISBN-13: 978-1-61521-120-3

Printed in the United States of America

18 17 16 15 14
7   6   5   4   3

CONTENTS

HOW TO USE THIS GUIDE

Along with all the volumes in the LIFECHANGE series of Bible studies, this guide to Daniel shares common goals:

1. To provide you with a firm foundation of understanding, plus a thirst to return to the book of Daniel throughout your life

2. To give you study patterns and skills that help you explore every part of the Bible

3. To offer you historical background, word definitions, and explanation notes to aid your study

4. To help you grasp as a whole the message of Daniel

5. To teach you how to let God's Word transform you into Christ's image

As You Begin

This guide includes twelve lessons that will take you chapter by chapter through all of Daniel. Each lesson is designed to take from one to two hours of preparation to complete on your own. To benefit most from this time, here's a good way to begin your work on each lesson:

1. Pray for God's help to keep you mentally alert and spiritually sensitive.

2. Read attentively the entire passage mentioned in the lesson's title. (You may want to read the passage from two or more Bible versions— perhaps at least once from a more literal translation such as the New International Version, English Standard Version, New American Standard Bible, or New King James Version, and perhaps once more in a paraphrase such as *The Message* or the New Living Translation.) Do your reading in an environment that's as free as possible from distractions. Allow your mind and heart to meditate on the words you encounter—words that are God's personal gift to you and to all His people.

After reading the passage, you're ready to dive into the numbered questions in this guide that make up the main portion of each lesson. Each of these questions is followed by blank space for writing your answers. (This act of writing your answers helps clarify your thinking and stimulates your mental engagement with the passage as well as your later recall.) Use extra paper or a notebook if the space for recording your answers seems too cramped. Continue through the questions in numbered order. If any question seems too difficult or unclear, just skip it and go on to the next.

Each of these questions will typically direct you back to Daniel to look again at a certain portion of the assigned passage for that lesson. (At this point, be sure to use a more literal Bible translation rather than a paraphrase.)

As you look closer at a passage, it's helpful to approach it in this progression:

Observe. What does the passage actually *say*? Ask God to help you see it clearly. Notice everything that's there.

Interpret. What does the passage *mean*? Ask God to help you understand. And remember that any passage's meaning is fundamentally determined by its *context*. So stay alert to all you'll see about the setting and background of Daniel, and keep thinking of this book as a whole while you proceed through it chapter by chapter. You'll be progressively building up your insights and familiarity with what it's all about.

Apply. Keep asking yourself, *How does this truth affect my life?* (Pray for God's help as you examine yourself in light of that truth and in light of His purpose for each passage.)

Try to consciously follow all three of these steps as you shape your written answer to each question in the lesson.

The Extras

In addition to the regular numbered questions you see in this guide, each lesson also offers several "optional" questions or suggestions that appear in the margins. All of these will appear under one of three headings:

Optional Application. These are suggested options for application. Consider these with prayerful sensitivity to the Lord's guidance.

For Thought and Discussion. Many of these questions address various ethical issues and other biblical principles that lead to a wide range of implications. They tend to be particularly suited for group discussion.

For Further Study. These often include cross-references to other parts of the Bible that shed light on a topic in the lesson, plus questions that delve deeper into the passage.

(For additional help for more effective Bible study, refer to the "Study Aids" section, starting on page 139.)

Changing Your Life

Don't let your study become an exercise in knowledge alone. Treat the passage as *God's* Word and stay in dialogue with Him as you study. Pray, "Lord, what do You want me to notice here?" "Father, why is this true?" "Lord, how does my life measure up to this?"

Let biblical truth sink into your inner convictions so you'll be increasingly able to act on this truth as a natural way of living.

At times, you may want to consider memorizing a certain verse or passage you come across in your study, one that particularly challenges or encourages you. To help with that, write down the words on a card to keep with you and set aside a few minutes each day to think about the passage. Recite it to yourself repeatedly, always thinking about its meaning. Return to it as often as you can, for a brief review. You'll soon find the words coming to mind spontaneously, and they'll begin to affect your motives and actions.

For Group Study

Exploring Scripture together in a group is especially valuable for the encouragement, support, and accountability it provides as you seek to apply God's Word to your life. Together you can listen jointly for God's guidance, pray for each other, help one another resist temptation, and share the spiritual principles you're learning to put into practice. Together you affirm that growing in faith, hope, and love is important and that you need each other in the process.

A group of four to ten people allows for the closest understanding of each other and the richest discussions in Bible study, but you can adapt this guide for other-sized groups. It will suit a wide range of group types, such as home Bible studies, growth groups, youth groups, and church classes. Both new and mature Christians will benefit from the guide, regardless of their previous experience in Bible study.

Aim for a positive atmosphere of acceptance, honesty, and openness. In your first meeting, explore candidly everyone's expectations and goals for your time together.

A typical schedule for group study is to take one lesson per week, but feel free to split lessons if you want to discuss them more thoroughly. Or omit some questions in a lesson if your preparation or discussion time is limited. (Group members can always study further on their own at a later time.)

When you come together, you probably won't have time to discuss all the questions in the lesson, so it's helpful for the leader to choose ahead of time the ones to be covered thoroughly. This is one of the main responsibilities a group leader typically assumes.

Each lesson in this guide ends with a section called "For the Group." It gives advice for that particular lesson on how to focus the discussion, how to apply the lesson to daily life, and so on. Reading each lesson's "For the Group" section ahead of time can help the leader be more effective in guiding the group.

You'll get the greatest benefit from your time together if each group member also prepares ahead of time by writing out his or her answers to each question in the lesson. The private reflection and prayer this preparation can stimulate will be especially important in helping everyone discern how God wants you to apply each lesson to your daily life.

There are many ways to structure the group meeting, and you may want to vary your routine occasionally to help keep things fresh.

Here are some of the elements you can consider including as you come together for each lesson:

Pray together. It's good to pause for prayer as you begin your time together as well as to incorporate a later, more extensive time of prayer for each other, after you've had time to share personal needs and prayer requests (you may want to write these down in a notebook). When you begin with prayer, it's worthwhile and honoring to God to ask especially for His Holy Spirit's guidance of your time together.

Worship. Some groups like to sing together and worship God with prayers of praise.

Review. You may want to take time to discuss what difference the previous week's lesson has made in your lives as well as recall the major emphasis you discovered in the passage for that week.

Read the passage aloud. Once you're ready to focus attention together on the assigned Scripture passage in this week's lesson, read it aloud. (One person could do this, or the reading could be shared.)

Open up for questions. Allow time for the group members to mention anything in the passage they may have particular questions about.

Summarize the passage. Have one or two people offer a summary of what the passage says.

Discuss. This will be the heart of your time together and will likely take the biggest portion of your time. Focus on the questions you see as the most important and most helpful. Allow and encourage everyone to be part of the discussion for each question. You may want to take written notes as the discussion proceeds. Ask follow-up questions to sharpen your attention and deepen your understanding of what you discuss. You may want to give special attention to the questions in the margin under the heading "For Thought and Discussion." Remember that sometimes these can be especially good for discussion, but be prepared for widely differing answers and opinions. As you hear each other, keep in mind each other's various backgrounds, personalities, and ways of thinking. You can practice godly discernment without ungodly judgment in your discussion.

Encourage further personal study. You can find more opportunities for exploring this lesson's themes and issues under the heading in the margin called "For Further Study" throughout the lesson. You can also pursue some of these together during your group time.

Focus on application. Look especially at the "Optional Application" listed in the margins throughout the lesson. Keep encouraging one another in the continual work of adjusting your lives to the truths God gives in Scripture.

Summarize your discoveries. You may want to read aloud through the passage one last time together, using the opportunity to solidify your understanding and appreciation of it and clarify how the Lord is speaking to you through it.

Look ahead. Glance together at the headings and questions in the next lesson to see what's coming next.

Give thanks to God. It's good to end your time together by pausing to express gratitude to God for His Word and the work of His Spirit in your minds and hearts during your time together.

Get to know each other better. In early sessions together, you may want to spend time establishing trust, common ground, and a sense of each other's background and what each person hopes to gain from the study. This may help you later with honest discussion about how the Bible applies to each of you. Understanding each other better will make it easier to share about personal applications.

Keep these worthy guidelines in mind throughout your time together:

> Let us consider how we may spur one another on toward love and good deeds.
> (HEBREWS 10:24)

> Carry each other's burdens, and in this way you will fulfill the law of Christ.
> (GALATIANS 6:2)

> Accept one another, then, just as Christ accepted you, in order to bring praise to God.
> (ROMANS 15:7)

THE BOOK OF DANIEL

Endurance for the Future

"Like Revelation, Daniel is essentially a book of pictures, appealing to our senses."[1]

"Although listed among the four major prophets of the Old Testament [along with Isaiah, Jeremiah, and Ezekiel], Daniel does not resemble the others because of its preponderance of narrative and apocalyptic material. Its length of twelve chapters is actually more similar to some of the minor prophets.

"Daniel gives the meaning of history more clearly than any other portion of the Bible and, what is more, it tells us how to live for God in ungodly times—like our own. Do many people regard Daniel as a clear revelation of the meaning of history—or of anything else for that matter? I doubt it! Yet that is what it is. . . .

"Consider these facts:

"1. Daniel was a godly man sent to live in ungodly Babylon at a time when God's blessing upon the Jewish nation seemed to have been withdrawn or postponed. This means that his position was much like that of believers trying to live in secular society today.

"2. The Babylon of Daniel's day was a type of all kingdoms that do not acknowledge God or think they can dispense with him. This is an apt description of most of the world in our time, including so-called 'Christian' America.

"3. Daniel (and his three friends Hananiah, Mishael, and Azariah) was under tremendous pressure to conform. That is, his religion was tolerated, even respected, as long as he did not allow it to intrude into public life or 'rock the ship' of state. That is our situation also. We can practice our religion so long as it is not in the schools, at work, or in any public place. We have to keep it 'on the reservation.'

"4. The world seemed to be winning. Nebuchadnezzar (and after him Belshazzar) reigned. Nebuchadnezzar believed himself to be above having to answer to anybody.

"5. Nevertheless, in spite of these things, God told Daniel that it is he, God, who is in control of history and that his purposes are being accomplished, even in the overthrow and captivity of his people. Moreover, in the end God will establish a kingdom that will endure forever. The destiny of the people of God is wrapped up in that eternal kingdom.

"I do not know of any message that is so timely and valuable for Christians living in our own secular and materialistic times as that message is."[2]

Theme

"The central theme of the book of Daniel is God's sovereignty over history and empires, setting up and removing kings as he pleases (2:21; 4:34-37). All of the kingdoms of this world will come to an end and will be replaced by the Lord's kingdom, which will never pass away (2:44; 7:27). Though trials and difficulties will continue for the saints up until the end, those who are faithful will be raised to glory, honor, and everlasting life in this final kingdom (12:1-3)."[3]

"The theme running through the whole book is that the fortunes of kings and the affairs of men are subject to God's decrees, and that he is able to accomplish his will despite the most determined opposition of the mightiest potentates on earth."[4]

"The things that appear in Daniel's visions . . . are very similar to the things portrayed in the Book of Revelation. The Book of Revelation cannot be properly interpreted without a general knowledge of the Book of Daniel. Material from every chapter of Daniel is either quoted or alluded to in Revelation, and only two chapters in Revelation do not have some background in Daniel."[5]

"What is the impact intended by the Holy Spirit upon the church through the message of this book? The predominant message is that God's people will experience suffering and be threatened with extinction, but that will not be the end of the story because their God is the living and all-powerful God who will get glory by vindicating his name and who will save them."[6]

Daniel the Man

"Daniel was a nobleman of Israel (possibly a prince) who was taken to Babylon in the first deportation (605 B.C.), probably while in his early teens (Daniel 1:3-4). His ministry lasted the entire length of the Babylonian Exile, his last dated prophecy being made in 536 B.C., when Daniel was in his eighties."[7]

Daniel's unique experiences made him particularly suitable for the special message he was given in this book, one with universal scope. Although the works of later prophets such as Ezekiel and Zechariah include references to blessing for all the world's peoples, "these prophetic books are Israel-centered and covenant-based. . . . What was lacking was a genuine world-view and a more comprehensive understanding of history, which would take account of other nations and their part in God's overarching purpose. This is where the book of Daniel comes into its own, and who could be better fitted to receive it than a well-instructed Jew who had lived the major part of his life as royal adviser in the court of the Babylonian world empire? His duties had forced him to break away from the thought-patterns of his childhood and, while maintaining his own faith, to see the application of its truths in an alien and powerful state. He lived through the fall of both the Assyrian and Babylonian empires, and in his old age would have been made ready to receive the visionary revelations concerning the final over-throw of God's enemies."[8]

Structure

"Daniel is probably the most highly organized book in Scripture. Some attribute this to the fact that near the end of his life, Daniel rewrote and organized the whole book into one consolidated message. The intricate arrangement of the ideas in the book demonstrates the extraordinary wisdom of Daniel (Daniel 1:17,19,20; 4:9; 5:11)."[9]

"The book is half narrative (chapters 1–6) and half visionary and apoca-lyptic writing (chapters 7–12).

"The narrative section tells stories about the Jewish community as it lived in exile in Babylon and Persia. The book revolves primarily around one of these exiles, Daniel, as we read about his career as a trusted adviser to three famous kings (Nebuchadnezzar, Belshazzar, and Darius).

"The visions of the future relate a double history—political history stretching from the time of Daniel through the Roman Empire and a more generalized, universal history recounting the struggle between forces of good and evil until the end of time.

"The issues with which the two halves of the book deal are universal, especially the following questions: How can followers of God maintain their loyalty to him while living in cultures that are hostile to biblical religion? What does the future hold, and how will history end?"[10]

"Chapters 2, 7, 8, 9, and 11 are to some extent parallel. They review a period of history by means of different symbols; in chapters 2 and 7 this period is identical, whereas in chapters 8, 9, and 11 the starting-point is later, and there is concentration on one theme. Chapter 2 is least complex; chapter 11 is very detailed."[11]

1. Sinclair Ferguson, *Daniel*, The Preacher's Commentary, ed. Lloyd J. Ogilvie (Nashville: Thomas Nelson, 1988), 134.
2. James Montgomery Boice, *Daniel* (Grand Rapids, MI: Baker, 2006), 9.
3. *ESV Study Bible* (Wheaton, IL: Crossway, 2008), introduction to Daniel, "Theme."
4. Gleason L. Archer Jr., *Daniel*, vol. 7, Expositor's Bible Commentary, ed. Frank E. Gaebelein (Grand Rapids, MI: Zondervan, 1985), 8.
5. *The Complete Word Study Old Testament*, ed. Warren Baker (Chattanooga, TN: AMG Publishers, 1994), introduction to Daniel.
6. Joyce G. Baldwin, *Daniel: An Introduction and Commentary*, vol. 25, Tyndale Old Testament Commentary (Downers Grove, IL: InterVarsity, 1978), 73–74.

7. *Complete Word Study,* introduction to Daniel.
8. Baldwin, 59.
9. *Complete Word Study,* introduction to Daniel.
10. Leland Ryken and Philip Graham Ryken, eds., *The Literary Study Bible* (Wheaton, IL: Crossway, 2007), introduction to Daniel, "The book at a glance."
11. Baldwin, 69.

DANIEL 1

A New Life in Babylon

1. For getting the most from Daniel, one of the best guidelines is found in 2 Timothy 3:16-17, words Paul wrote with the Old Testament first in view. He said that *all* Scripture is of great benefit to (a) teach us, (b) rebuke us, (c) correct us, and (d) train us in righteousness. Paul added that these Scriptures completely equip the person of God "for every good work" (verse 17). As you think seriously about those guidelines, in which of these areas do you especially want to experience the usefulness of Daniel? Express your desire in a written prayer to God.

_____

_____

_____

_____

2. In Jeremiah 23:29, God says that His Word is like fire and like a hammer. He can use the Scriptures to burn away unclean thoughts and misdirected desires in our hearts. He can also use Scripture, with hammer-like hardness, to crush and crumble our spiritual hardness. From your study of Daniel, how do you most want to see the "fire and hammer" power of God's Word at work in your life? Again, express this longing in a written prayer to God.

Optional Application: After Jesus' resurrection, when He was explaining Old Testament passages to His disciples, we read that He "opened their minds so they could understand the Scriptures" (Luke 24:45). Ask God to do that kind of work in *your* mind as you study Daniel so you're released and free to learn everything here He wants you to learn and so you can become as bold and worshipful and faithful as those early disciples of Jesus. Express this desire to Him in prayer.

_____

_____

_____

_____

3. Think about these words of Paul to his younger helper Timothy: "Do your best to present yourself to God as one approved, a worker who does not need to be ashamed and who correctly handles the word of truth" (2 Timothy 2:15). As you study God's truth in Daniel, he calls you to be a "worker." It takes *work*—concentration and perseverance—to fully appropriate God's blessings for us. Express here your commitment before God to work diligently in this study of Daniel.

_____

_____

_____

_____

4. Glance through the pages of Daniel and briefly scan each chapter. What are your overall impressions of the book, including its structure and themes?

_____

_____

_____

_____

5. Now turn your focus to the first chapter of Daniel. What important background events are given in verses 1-2?

_____

_____

_____

_____

In the third year of the reign of Jehoiakim (1:1).
That is, 605 BC.

***Nebuchadnezzar king of Babylon came to
Jerusalem and besieged it*** (1:1). See 2 Kings
23:36–24:6. "This was the first of three inva-
sions of Judah by Nebuchadnezzar. The second
was in 597 B.C. (2 Kings 24:1-14), and the third
in 587 B.C. (2 Kings 25:1-24)."[1]

6. Notice the action attributed to God in Daniel
   1:2. In its context here, how does this help
   us understand God's sovereignty and His
   purposes?

   _____

   _____

   _____

   _____

   _____

***Along with some of the articles from the temple
of God. These he [Nebuchadnezzar] carried
off to the temple of his god in Babylonia***
(1:2). "Jews boasted that their God, Jehovah,
was all-powerful. Nebuchadnezzar believed
that he was greater than that God. So when he
forced the capitulation of Jerusalem, his cause
and his gods seemed vindicated. It was in
demonstration of that conviction that he
brought the gold and silver articles that had
been dedicated to the service of Jehovah in
Jerusalem to Babylon to be placed in the treasure house of his gods. The heathen gods had
triumphed! Nebuchadnezzar was sovereign! In
this case, as in so many other historical situa-
tions, appearances were deceiving."[2]

7. What are the most significant details we learn
   about Daniel and his three fellow exiles in
   1:3-7?

17

For Further Study: In 2 Kings 24–25, what do you feel are the most important background elements for the book of Daniel?

Israelites from the royal family and the nobility (1:3). Nebuchadnezzar had brought these captives back to Babylon after his attack on Jerusalem. "This deportation was the beginning of what came to be known as the Babylonian exile, which was the result of the Lord's judgment on his people. In Lev. 26:33,39 the Lord threatened his people with exile if they were unfaithful to the terms of the covenant established at Mount Sinai (see also Deut. 4:27; 28:64). After a lengthy history of disobedience, this threat was carried out in several stages, culminating in the destruction of Jerusalem and the burning of the temple in 586 B.C. The final destruction and exile were foreshadowed by this earlier exile."[3]

They were to enter the king's service (1:5). "Somewhat like Alexander the great at a later time, Nebuchadnezzar adopted an enlightened policy of enlisting the most promising young men of his new empire into government service, whatever their nationality. . . . Nebuchadnezzar resolved to pool the best brains and abilities discoverable in the ranks of the nations he had conquered."[4]

Daniel, Hananiah, Mishael and Azariah (1:6). "The Jewish names of these men each contains a name of God and has a spiritual meaning. Daniel and Mishael both contain the syllable *el*, which means 'God' and is the basis of the frequently appearing (plural) name *Elohim*. Daniel means 'God is my Judge.' Mishael means 'Who is like God?' The other two names, Hananiah and Azariah, both contain a shortened form of the name Jehovah. Hananiah means 'Jehovah is gracious.' Azariah means 'Jehovah is my helper.' The very names of these men were reminders of their heritage

18

and a challenge to them to remain faithful to the Lord."[5]

New names (1:7). "The exiles were given names linked with Babylonian deities in place of Israelite names linked with their God. Daniel ('God is my Judge'), Hananiah ('Yahweh is gracious'), Mishael ('Who is what God is?'), and Azariah ('Yahweh is a helper') became names that invoked the help of the Babylonian gods Marduk, Bel, and Nebo: Belteshazzar ('O Lady [wife of the god Bel], protect the king!'), Shadrach ('I am very fearful [of God]' or 'command of Aku [the moon god]'), Meshach ('I am of little account' or 'Who is like Aku?'), and Abednego ('servant of the shining one [Nebo]')."[6]

To Daniel, the name Belteshazzar (1:7). See Nebuchadnezzar's explanation of this in 4:8.

In Daniel, "each of the first six chapters consists of a self-contained ordeal story."[7]

---

8. How would you summarize what Daniel was trying to "prove" by the kind of testing he pursued in 1:8-16?

_____

_____

_____

_____

Not to defile himself with the royal food and wine (1:8). A likely explanation: "Daniel and his friends avoided the luxurious diet of the king's table as a way of protecting themselves from being ensnared by the temptations of the Babylonian culture. They used their distinctive diet as a way of retaining their distinctive identity as Jewish exiles and avoiding complete assimilation into Babylonian culture (which

For Thought and Discussion: From the perspective of these four young Jewish men of noble heritage introduced to us in Daniel 1, what is most different about their routines and experiences in Babylon from what these would have been if they were still in their home-land and Babylon had never defeated Jerusalem?

For Further Study: When you compare these opening verses of Daniel with chapter 39 of Isaiah, what connections do you see, including fulfillment of prophecy?

Optional Application: We read in Daniel 1:8 of what "Daniel resolved" to do. Think about his example in this. What are some important resolutions that you have made in your Christian life? What need might there be now in your life for a further resolution of some kind?

19

was the king's goal with these conquered subjects). With this restricted diet they continually reminded themselves, in this time of testing, that they were the people of God in a foreign land and that they were dependent for their food, indeed for their very lives, upon God, their Creator, not King Nebuchadnezzar."[8]

For Thought and Discussion: Imagine yourself as the chief official mentioned in 1:8-14, who is confronted by this bold request from Daniel and his friends. What are the various factors that might cause you to agree to this "test" that Daniel proposed, despite the objections mentioned in verse 10?

"As always, small things (questions of diet) gesture toward larger issues (paganism versus loyalty to God)."[9]

9. What were the most significant obstacles Daniel had to overcome in verses 8-16?

_____

_____

_____

_____

For Further Study: How does Daniel 1:9 indicate an answer to the prayer request of Solomon, centuries earlier, as given in 1 Kings 8:50?

10. Notice the action attributed to God in verse 9. In its context here, what does this communicate about God's grace and His sovereign purposes?

_____

_____

_____

_____

Optional Application: Reflect further on the "test" Daniel pursued in 1:8-16. What would be an example of how some similar testing would be appropriate for you to pursue in your own life?

11. What do you find most impressive about the character and capabilities of Daniel and his three fellow exiles as they're described in verses 17-20?

_____

_____

_____

_____

12. Notice the action attributed to God in verse 17. What does it communicate about God's grace and His gifting for His people?

_____

_____

_____

_____

At the end of the time set by the king to bring them into his service (1:18). After three years (recall verse 5).

So they entered the king's service (1:19). "God placed them in a unique position where they could be a blessing to their captors and build up the society in which they found themselves (see Jeremiah 29:5-7), while at the same time enabling them to remain true to him amid extraordinary pressures."[10]

Ten times better than all the magicians and enchanters (1:20). "Whatever means these royal advisers used to gain knowledge, Daniel and his friends were able to demonstrate superior insight on the matters they were questioned about."[11]

13. Note especially the brief fact mentioned in the final verse of this chapter. What is the significance of this fact being mentioned so early in the book rather than at the end of it?

_____

_____

_____

_____

The first year of King Cyrus (1:21). That is, 539 BC, nearly seven decades after the events mentioned in verse 1. "Daniel was one of the first

Optional Application: What aspects of Daniel's character, as shown in this chapter, do you believe are strengths that God, by His grace, wants to further develop in your life? How is God already working on this in your life, and how does He want you to respond to His training?

captives taken to Babylonia, and he lived to see the first exiles return to Jerusalem in 538 B.C. Throughout this time he honored God, and God honored him. While serving as a counselor to the kings of Babylonia, Daniel was God's spokesman to the Babylonian Empire. Babylonia was a wicked nation, but it would have been much worse without Daniel's influence."[12]

14. How is Daniel's leadership demonstrated in this chapter?

_____

_____

_____

_____

15. In Daniel 1, what would you select as the key verse or passage—one that best captures or reflects the dynamics of what this chapter is all about?

_____

_____

_____

16. List any lingering questions you have about Daniel 1.

_____

_____

_____

_____

For the Group

(In your first meeting, it may be helpful to turn to the front of this book and review together the

22

sections titled "How to Use This Guide" and "For Group Study.")

You may want to focus your discussion for lesson 1 especially on the following issues, themes, and concepts. (These things will likely reflect what group members have learned in their individual study of this week's passage, although they'll also have made discoveries in other areas as well.)

- The holiness of God's people
- Our dependence on God
- True heroism
- Godliness
- Perseverance
- God's faithfulness
- God's sovereignty over all things

The following numbered questions in lesson 1 may stimulate your best and most helpful discussion: 4, 8, 9, 11, 14, 15, and 16.

Look also at the questions in the margin under the heading "For Thought and Discussion."

1. *New Geneva Study Bible* (Nashville: Thomas Nelson, 1995), at Daniel 1:1.
2. James Montgomery Boice, *Daniel* (Grand Rapids, MI: Baker, 2006), 15.
3. *ESV Study Bible* (Wheaton, IL: Crossway, 2008), at Daniel 1:1-2.
4. Gleason L. Archer Jr., *Daniel*, vol. 7, Expositor's Bible Commentary, ed. Frank E. Gaebelein (Grand Rapids, MI: Zondervan, 1985), 33.
5. Boice, 21.
6. *ESV*, at Daniel 1:5-7.
7. Leland Ryken and Philip Graham Ryken, eds., *The Literary Study Bible* (Wheaton, IL: Crossway, 2007), at Daniel 2.
8. *ESV*, at Daniel 1:8-16.
9. Ryken and Ryken, at Daniel 1.
10. *ESV*, at Daniel 1:17-21.
11. *New Geneva*, at Daniel 1:20.
12. *Life Application Bible*, various editions (Wheaton, IL: Tyndale, 1988 and later), at Daniel 1:21.

DANIEL 2

The King's Troubling Dream

1. a. In the exchanges between Nebuchadnezzar and his royal officials in Daniel 2:1-11, what does Nebuchadnezzar seek and how does he pursue this?

_____

_____

_____

b. How would you summarize the series of responses from the royal officials?

_____

_____

_____

_____

c. What reasons can you think of for why Nebuchadnezzar refused to reveal the details of his dream?

_____

_____

_____

In the second year of his reign, Nebuchadnezzar (2:1). 604 BC.

Dreams (2:1). "Dreams were considered messages from the gods, and the wise men were expected to interpret them. Usually these wise men could give some sort of interpretation as long as they knew what the dream was about."[1]

Astrologers (2:2). Or, more literally, "Chaldeans" (ESV, NASB, NKJV). "Here 'Chaldeans' probably means a class of soothsayers and astrologers, rather than the name of an ethnic group."[2]

In Aramaic (Footnote). From this point forward through all of chapter 7, the original text is in the Aramaic (the international language of the day and common language of this region) rather than Hebrew. A possible explanation: "These six chapters deal with matters of importance to the Gentile nations of the Near East and were written in a language understandable to all. But the last five chapters (8–12) revert to Hebrew, since they deal with special concerns of the chosen people."[3] (Also written originally in Aramaic are these passages: Ezra 4:8–6:18; 7:12-26; Jeremiah 10:11.) "By New Testament times, Aramaic had become the common language of Palestine."[4]

2. In your own words, summarize the situation as it develops in verses 12-13.

_____

_____

_____

_____

3. What do you find most significant about Daniel's response in verses 14-16?

_____

_____

_____

4. What do you find most significant about Daniel's response in verses 17-18?

_____

_____

_____

_____

Optional Application: Notice again Daniel's focus on prayer in 2:17-18. What specific needs, burdens, and desires in your life are worthy of the kind of prayer for God's mercy that Daniel called for in these verses?

Plead for mercy from the God of heaven (2:18). "Daniel . . . realized that human wisdom was insufficient to meet the king's demand. Only divine revelation could provide the answer."[5]

God of heaven (2:18). "It is interesting that the word 'LORD' ('Yahweh' or 'Jehovah') does not appear in the Aramaic section [Daniel 2:4 through the end of chapter 7]. Instead expressions like the 'King of heaven' (4:37) or 'high God' (4:2,24) are used in order to distinguish Him from the gods of the pagans."[6]

Mystery (2:18). "A key word in Daniel. . . . The Greek equivalent is used in the New Testament to refer to the secret purposes of God that he reveals only to his chosen prophets and apostles."[7] See also verses 19, 27-30, and 47 in this chapter as well as 4:9.

5. In verse 19, what is especially noteworthy about the way God responded to this situation?

_____

_____

_____

6. What do verses 20-23 reveal about Daniel's perspective of what has happened?

_____

_____

For Further Study:
Reflect on the attri-
butes of God that
Daniel praises in
verses 20-22. How do
you see these also
reflected in these
passages: 1 Samuel
2:7-8; 1 Chronicles
29:11-12; Job 28:20-
28; Psalm 25:14; 36:9;
75:4-7; 139:11-12;
Proverbs 2:6-7; Isaiah
44:7-8; Jeremiah
27:5-7; 32:17-20; Amos
3:7; Hebrews 4:12-13;
James 1:5,17; 3:15-17.

**Optional
Application:** Notice
especially the things
Daniel praises God
for in Daniel 2:20-
23. What particular
reasons do you have
for praising God for
these same things?

**For Thought and
Discussion:** Imagine
yourself as Arioch,
the commander of
the king's guard
mentioned in
Daniel 2:14-15 and
24-25. Throughout
this episode, what
might be your
strongest impres-
sions of (a) King
Nebuchadnezzar,
(b) the king's wise
men, and (c) Daniel?

7. Summarize the developments that occur in
verses 24-26.

_____

_____

_____

_____

Do not execute the wise men (2:24). "Daniel did
not use his success merely to promote his own
self-interest. He also thought of others."[8]

8. In verses 27-30, what are the most important
points Daniel makes in his reply to the king?

_____

_____

_____

_____

9. What are the major features of the king's dream
that Daniel mentions in verses 31-35?

_____

_____

_____

_____

*The head . . . made of pure gold, its chest
and arms of silver, its belly and thighs of
bronze, its legs of iron, its feet partly of
iron and partly of baked clay* (2:32-33).
Representing four kingdoms, as Daniel's interpretation makes clear (see verses 36-43). "The

four kingdoms have been widely understood since Josephus (1st century A.D.) to be the empires of Babylon, Medo-Persia, Greece, and Rome."[9]

A rock . . . struck the statue on its feet (2:34). "The stone, which most agree represents Christ and His rule . . . strikes only the feet, but the whole image is crushed [2:35]. . . . The crushing of the whole image teaches that Christ's reign will put an end to all forms of human government."[10]

The rock that struck the statue became a huge mountain and filled the whole earth (2:35). See the interpretation in verse 44. "The heavenly world breaks in . . . to consume human kingdoms and to bestow in their place one heavenly kingdom which will fill the earth."[11]

10. Summarize how Daniel interprets each feature of the king's dream as narrated in verses 36-45.

_____

_____

_____

_____

We will interpret it (2:36). "When Daniel says 'we,' he is referring to himself and his three friends. Just as he involved them in praying for God's help, he gave them credit when he presented the interpretation."[12]

That head of gold (2:38). "A fitting description" for Nebuchadnezzar; under him, "the nation had become a vast empire, and Nebuchadnezzar ruled ruthlessly. Babylon itself was an amazing achievement, with its hanging gardens, many temples, and a bridge crossing the Euphrates River."[13]

For Further Study:
What parallels do you see between Daniel's story in this chapter and the story of Joseph in Genesis 41?

"It is striking that God gave this dream to Nebuchadnezzar in the seventh century B.C. (about 602), for in this dream and in the subsequent visions linked to it in chapters 7 and 8, God predicts in accurate detail the future kingdoms that would arise to dominate world history in the sixth, fourth, and first centuries B.C. . . . In the dream . . . each kingdom has its own glory but also its own end: both have been assigned to it by God. The progression of world history is typically not upward to glory and unity but rather downward to dishonor and disunity."[14]

11. Summarize the king's response in verses 46-48 to Daniel's interpretation of the dream.

   _____

   _____

   _____

   _____

12. What additional detail is narrated in verse 49, and what is its significance?

   _____

   _____

   _____

   _____

13. How is Daniel's leadership demonstrated in this chapter?

   _____

   _____

_____

_____

14. What most impresses you in this chapter about Daniel's understanding of God?

_____

_____

_____

_____

15. In Daniel 2, what would you select as the key verse or passage—one that best captures or reflects the dynamics of what this chapter is all about?

_____

_____

_____

_____

16. List any lingering questions you have about Daniel 2.

_____

_____

_____

_____

Optional Application: What aspects of Daniel's character, as shown in this chapter, do you believe are strengths that God, by His grace, wants to further develop in your life? How is God already working on this in your life, and how does He want you to respond to His training?

For the Group

You may want to focus your discussion for lesson 2 especially on the following issues, themes, and concepts. (These will likely reflect what group members have learned in their individual study of this week's passage, although they'll also have made discoveries in other areas as well.)

- Our dependence on God
- God's sovereignty over all things

- True heroism
- Godliness
- Perseverance
- God's faithfulness
- Wisdom

The following numbered questions in lesson 2 may stimulate your best and most helpful discussion: 5, 6, 8, 13, 14, 15, and 16.

Look also at the questions in the margin under the heading "For Thought and Discussion."

1. *Life Application Bible*, various editions (Wheaton, IL: Tyndale, 1988 and later), at Daniel 2:1-11.
2. *New Geneva Study Bible* (Nashville: Thomas Nelson, 1995), at Daniel 2:2.
3. *NIV Study Bible* (Grand Rapids, MI: Zondervan, 1985), at Daniel 2:4.
4. *The Complete Word Study Old Testament*, ed. Warren Baker (Chattanooga, TN: AMG Publishers, 1994), at Daniel 2:4.
5. *New Geneva*, at Daniel 2:18.
6. *Complete Word Study*, at Daniel 2:4.
7. *NIV*, at Daniel 2:18.
8. *Life Application*, at Daniel 2:24.
9. *New Geneva*, at Daniel 2:37-40.
10. *Complete Word Study*, at Daniel 2:31-45.
11. Joyce G. Baldwin, *Daniel: An Introduction and Commentary*, vol. 25, Tyndale Old Testament Commentary (Downers Grove, IL: InterVarsity, 1978), 61.
12. *Life Application,* at Daniel 2:36.
13. *ESV Study Bible* (Wheaton, IL: Crossway, 2008), at Daniel 2:37-38.
14. *ESV,* at Daniel 2:43-44.

LESSON THREE

DANIEL 3

Tested by Fire

"Daniel drops out of the story momentarily as the action shifts to Daniel's three
friends. . . . The episode is a paradigm of
Israel's experience in exile: God is with
them in the furnace, where they are
called to faithfulness."[1]

For Thought and Discussion: In the past, what have been your strongest impressions of this story about the three young Hebrew men thrown into a furnace of fire?

1. In the narrative of chapter 3, notice the repetition of a couple of lists: first in verses 2 and 3 and then in verses 5, 7, 10, and 15. What is the effect of this repetition in the story's impact?

_____

_____

_____

_____

2. What are the most important details given in verses 1-7?

_____

_____

_____

_____

"A Babylonian document from the time of Nebuchadnezzar (605–562 B.C.) warns not to harm the statue that had been set up: 'Beside my statue as king … I wrote an inscription mentioning my name … I erected for posterity. May future kings respect the monument, remember the praise of the gods. . . . He who respects … my royal name, who does not abrogate my statutes and not change my decrees, his throne shall be secure, his life last long, his dynasty shall continue.'"[2]

On the plain of Dura in the province of Babylon (3:1). "Probably about six miles south of Babylon."[3] The statue's "location on a plain in Babylon recalls the location of the Tower of Babel (also on a plain, Genesis 11:2), as does its purpose to provide a unifying center for all the peoples of the earth."[4]

Blazing furnace (3:6). "Furnaces or kilns were used in Babylon for firing bricks (Genesis 11:3)."[5]

---

3. What is the substance of the accusation made in verses 8-12, and why is it such a serious charge?

_____

_____

_____

_____

Some Jews . . . Shadrach, Meshach and Abednego (3:12). "Daniel himself is curiously absent; perhaps he is away on a mission, or perhaps above the administrative rulers mentioned in 3:3 and thus immune from such displays of Nebuchadnezzar's pride, or perhaps the Chaldeans did not feel safe accusing Daniel."[6]

4. What is revealed most about Nebuchadnezzar in his response as recorded in verses 13-15?

_____

_____

_____

_____

"If you are ready to fall down and worship the image I made," King Nebuchadnezzar told these three young men, "very good" (3:15). "The three men had one more chance. Here are eight excuses they could have used to bow to the statue and save their lives:

"(1) We will bow down but not actually *worship* the idol.

"(2) We won't become idol worshipers, but will do this one time, then ask God for forgiveness.

"(3) The king has absolute power and we must obey him. God will understand.

"(4) The king appointed us — we owe this to him.

"(5) This is a foreign land, so God will excuse us for following the customs of the land.

"(6) Our ancestors set up idols in God's temple! This isn't half as bad!

"(7) We're not hurting anybody.

"(8) If we get ourselves killed and some heathens take our high positions, they won't help our people in exile!

"Although all these excuses sound sensible at first, they are dangerous. To bow to the image would violate God's command in Exodus 20:3, 'You shall have no other gods before me.' It would also erase their testimony for God forever. Never again could they talk about the power of their God above all other gods.

"What excuses do you use for not standing up for God?"[7]

5. In verses 16-18, what do you see as the most significant elements in the response to the king from these three men?

_____

_____

_____

_____

6. In what happens next (see verses 19-23), what are the most important details?

_____

_____

_____

_____

Seven times hotter (3:19). This expression "may have been figurative for 'as hot as possible' (seven signifies completeness)."[8]

---

7. The amazing developments in verses 24-25 are narrated from King Nebuchadnezzar's viewpoint. What are the reasons for his astonishment, and what does this reveal about him?

_____

_____

_____

_____

Like a son of the gods (3:25). See also verse 28. "Nebuchadnezzar was speaking as a pagan polytheist and was content to conceive of the fourth figure as a lesser heavenly being sent by the all-powerful God of the Israelites."[9] "The identity of the fourth figure has been a subject of dispute. Since the earliest days, Christians have held that it was a preincarnate appearance of Jesus Christ. This is supported by the fact that Daniel uses 'Son of man' in Daniel 7:13 in connection with divine glory. This gives the use of 'Son of God' a similar weight by implication."[10]

The Most High God (3:26). "This is a title expressing God's universal authority. As in verse 29 and 2:47, such a confession on the lips of a pagan is not an acknowledgment that Daniel's Lord is the only God, but only that He is supreme over other gods (4:2,17,34). To a Jew it means there is only one God (4:24-32; 5:18,21; 7:18-27)."[11]

8. How is God's miraculous protection of the three men emphasized in verses 26-27?

_____

_____

_____

_____

9. How fully do you think Nebuchadnezzar's words in verse 28 are also reflective of *God's* perspective on what has just happened?

_____

_____

_____

_____

10. What else does Nebuchadnezzar do in his response to this amazing incident, according to verses 29-30?

_____

_____

_____

_____

For Further Study: How is the reality of what happens in Daniel 3:25 reflected in the words of Psalm 91:9-12 and Isaiah 43:1-2?

For Further Study: In Daniel 3:28, the king refers to the fourth figure he saw walking inside the fiery furnace as the "angel" of the God of Shadrach, Meshach, and Abednego. How does this figure compare with the "angel of the LORD" we see in these passages: Genesis 16:1-11; 22:11-15; Exodus 3:2; Numbers 22:22-35; Judges 2:1-4; 6:11-12,21-22; 13:3-21; 2 Samuel 24:16; 1 Kings 19:7; 2 Kings 1:3,15; 19:35; Psalm 34:7; 35:5-6.

What character qualities of Shadrach, Meshach, and Abednego do you believe are strengths that God, by His grace, wants to further develop in your life? How is God already working on this in your life, and how does He want you to respond to His training?

11. In Daniel 3, what would you select as the key verse or passage—one that best captures or reflects the dynamics of what this chapter is all about?

_____

_____

_____

_____

12. List any lingering questions you have about Daniel 3.

_____

_____

_____

_____

For the Group

You may want to focus your discussion for lesson 3 especially on the following issues, themes, and concepts. (These will likely reflect what group members have learned in their individual study of this week's passage, although they'll also have made discoveries in other areas as well.)

- Our dependence on God
- God's sovereignty over all things
- True heroism
- Godliness
- Perseverance
- God's faithfulness
- Pride and humility

The following numbered questions in lesson 3 may stimulate your best and most helpful discussion: 4, 7, 9, 11, and 12.

Remember to look also at the "For Thought and Discussion" questions in the margin.

1. Leland Ryken and Philip Graham Ryken, eds., *The Literary Study Bible* (Wheaton, IL: Crossway, 2007), at Daniel 3.
2. *ESV Study Bible* (Wheaton, IL: Crossway, 2008), at Daniel 3:1-30.
3. *New Geneva Study Bible* (Nashville: Thomas Nelson, 1995), at Daniel 3:1.
4. *ESV*, at Daniel 3:1.
5. *New Geneva*, at Daniel 3:6.
6. *ESV*, at Daniel 3:12.
7. *Life Application Bible*, various editions (Wheaton, IL: Tyndale, 1988 and later), at Daniel 3:15.
8. *NIV Study Bible* (Grand Rapids, MI: Zondervan, 1985), at Daniel 3:19.
9. *NIV*, at Daniel 3:25.
10. *The Complete Word Study Old Testament*, ed. Warren Baker (Chattanooga, TN: AMG Publishers, 1994), at Daniel 3:25.
11. *New Geneva*, at Daniel 3:26.

DANIEL 4

The Humiliation of a King

1. Proverbs 2:1-5 tells about the sincere person who truly longs for wisdom and understanding and who searches the Scriptures for it as if there were treasure buried there. Such a person, this passage says, will come to understand the fear of the Lord and discover the knowledge of God. As you continue exploring Daniel, what "buried treasure" would you like God to help you find here to show you what God and His wisdom are really like? If you have this desire, how would you express it in your own words of prayer to God?

   _____

   _____

   _____

   _____

2. As an introduction to the events of this chapter, what are the major truths that Nebuchadnezzar declares in verses 1-3?

   _____

   _____

   _____

   _____

For Thought and Discussion: Notice Nebuchadnezzar's words in Daniel 4:4 about being "at home in my palace, contented and prosperous." How easy is it to identify here with this ancient Near Eastern monarch?

"The narrative [in Daniel 4] begins at the end of the story, with the letter of praise to God that Nebuchadnezzar wrote after his recovery."[1] "Nebuchadnezzar reached this conclusion after the experiences of verses 4-37. The language of his confession may reflect Daniel's influence."[2]

Signs and wonders that the Most High God has performed for me (4:2). "From becoming a persecutor of the faithful, Nebuchadnezzar has himself become a witness to the faith."[3]

---

3. What are the important details, from Nebuchadnezzar's perspective, that the king highlights in his narrative in verses 4-7?

_____

_____

_____

_____

4. What do verses 8-9 emphasize regarding Nebuchadnezzar's view of the man Daniel?

_____

_____

_____

_____

The spirit of the holy gods (4:8). "Nebuchadnezzar . . . may have been thinking of another god known to him rather than the God of Daniel."[4]

---

5. What are the significant details of his dream that the king reveals in verses 10-12?

_____

_____

_____

_____

Tree (4:10). See Daniel's interpretation of this in
  verses 20-22.

6. What further significant details of his
   dream does Nebuchadnezzar reveal in verses
   13-16?

   _____

   _____

   _____

A messenger (4:13). Or, more literally, "watcher"
  (ESV, NASB, NKJV). Likewise in verse 23 and 17.

Seven times (4:16). Or "seven periods of time" (ESV,
  NASB). "The text does not explain the length of
  time, but 'seven' signifies completion and most
  ancient and modern scholars have argued it
  was 'seven years.'"[5]

7. Summarize in your own words the emphatic
   statements in verse 17.

   _____

   _____

   _____

8. What elements of the king's view of Daniel are
   emphasized in verse 18?

For Further Study:
How do you see Daniel's service to King Nebuchadnezzar as a reflection of the principles taught later by the apostle Paul in Ephesians 6:5-8?

_____

_____

_____

_____

9. How does verse 19 highlight the seriousness of the king's dream?

_____

_____

_____

_____

"Nebuchadnezzar was the man who had destroyed Jerusalem and carried Daniel away in his service. However, when Daniel received a message from God of judgment upon Nebuchadnezzar, he urged Nebuchadnezzar to repent (4:27) in hopes that the consequences could be avoided."[6]

10. In verses 20-26, what are the main points Daniel makes in his interpretation of the dream?

_____

_____

_____

_____

Leave the stump, bound with iron and bronze (4:23). "Possibly suggesting that Nebuchadnezzar's kingdom would be protected and then established after he learned to honor the true God."[7]

44

Until you acknowledge that the Most High is sovereign (4:25). "The purpose of Nebuchadnezzar's humiliation was to compel him to recognize God's sovereignty."[8]

11. How would you construe in your own words the further counsel Daniel gives the king in verse 27?

_____

_____

_____

_____

Renounce your sins by doing what is right, and your wickedness by being kind to the oppressed (4:27). "Daniel (a Jew who believed in the one true God) was willing to tell Nebuchadnezzar (a pagan king) that he should conform to moral standards that Daniel had learned from God. This appeal to repentance implied that the fate depicted for Nebuchadnezzar in the dream was not inevitable, and it provided Nebuchadnezzar with an opportunity to repent of his pride. If Nebuchadnezzar humbled himself, God would not need to humble him further. Even pagan rulers are accountable to the God of the Bible."[9]

Twelve months later (4:29). "Daniel pleaded with Nebuchadnezzar to change his ways [verse 27], and God gave him twelve months in which to do it. Unfortunately, there was no repentance in the heart of this proud king, and so the dream was fulfilled."[10]

"The struggle between Nebuchadnezzar and God, recorded in Daniel, is actually only one example of that greater struggle between the world's way of doing things and God's way of doing things, which has

For Further Study: How does the use of the "tree" imagery in Daniel 4 compare with its representation of Assyria in Ezekiel 31? Compare also Psalm 1:3; 37:35; 52:8; 92:12; Jeremiah 11:16-17; 17:8.

For Thought and Discussion: Imagine yourself in King Nebuchadnezzar's position after hearing Daniel's interpretation of the strange dream and then going month after month without seeing anything take place that Daniel had predicted. What thoughts might be going through your mind?

prevailed at all times and prevails today. It is this that makes Daniel a contemporary book."[11]

12. In verses 28-33, what is most significant in the description of how the king's dream became reality?

_____

_____

_____

_____

Is not this the great Babylon I have built as the royal residence, by my mighty power and for the glory of my majesty? (4:30). "This is a true statement in one sense. Nebuchadnezzar had built Babylon, and he had undoubtedly done it for his own glory. But in forgetting God, who had given him the opportunity to create such magnificence, Nebuchadnezzar was actually taking God's glory to himself. Like all secular humanists, he was saying that all that exists is *of* man, *by* man, and *for* man's glory."[12]

He was driven away from people (4:33). It is possible "that Daniel watched over the Empire during the time when these consequences took place (4:28-37)."[13]

---

13. From all that he experienced, what did King Nebuchadnezzar learn most about God, according to his words in verses 34-37?

_____

_____

_____

_____

The King of heaven (4:37). "This unique title brings together the theme of the chapter: the rule of God from heaven." The word for heaven (also translated as "sky") is used in verses 11, 12, 13, 15, 20, 21, 22, 23, 25, 26, 31, 33, 34, 35, and 37.

"Nebuchadnezzar's confession ... communicates the central theme of the Book of Daniel, namely, the absolute sovereignty of the God of Israel. ... Although Nebuchadnezzar confesses God's sovereignty, he does not confess a belief that the God of Israel is the only God."[14]

14. In Daniel 4, what would you select as the key verse or passage—one that best captures or reflects the dynamics of what this chapter is all about?

_____

_____

_____

_____

15. List any lingering questions you have about Daniel 4.

_____

_____

_____

_____

For the Group

You may want to focus your discussion for lesson 4 especially on the following issues, themes, and concepts. (These will likely reflect what group members have learned in their individual study of this week's passage, although they'll also have made discoveries in other areas as well.)

- Our dependence on God
- God's sovereignty over all things
- True heroism
- Godliness
- Wisdom
- Pride and humility
- Worship

The following numbered questions in lesson 4 may stimulate your best and most helpful discussion: 2, 9, 10, 11, 13, 14, and 15.

Remember to look also at the "For Thought and Discussion" questions in the margin.

1. *ESV Study Bible* (Wheaton, IL: Crossway, 2008), at Daniel 4:1-3.
2. *NIV Study Bible* (Grand Rapids, MI: Zondervan, 1985), at Daniel 4:1-3.
3. *ESV*, at Daniel 4:1-3.
4. *New Geneva Study Bible* (Nashville: Thomas Nelson, 1995), at Daniel 4:8.
5. *ESV*, at Daniel 4:16.
6. *The Complete Word Study Old Testament*, ed. Warren Baker (Chattanooga, TN: AMG Publishers, 1994), at Daniel 4:19.
7. *ESV*, at Daniel 4:23.
8. *New Geneva,* at Daniel 4:25.
9. *ESV*, at Daniel 4:26.
10. *Life Application Bible*, various editions (Wheaton, IL: Tyndale, 1988 and later), at Daniel 4:27-33.
11. James Montgomery Boice, *Daniel* (Grand Rapids, MI: Baker, 2006), 16.
12. Boice, 16.
13. *Complete Word Study*, at Daniel 4:29.
14. *New Geneva,* at Daniel 4:3; 4:34,35,37.

DANIEL 5

Belshazzar's Feast

"In an episode rich in atmosphere, the scene of action is the luxurious and decadent court of Belshazzar, with the decadence rendered all the more abhorrent by the desecration of the vessels that had been plundered from the temple in Jerusalem (verses 2-4). The episode turns into a phantasmagoria of shocking events, beginning with a disembodied hand that writes a mysterious message on the wall. Daniel steps into the horror with his characteristic confidence and charisma, interpreting the dream and announcing God's judgment against the evil king."[1]

1. What is the setting for this chapter, as presented in verse 1?

   _____

   _____

   _____

   _____

Belshazzar (5:1). "From Babylonian sources we know that Belshazzar was placed in charge of affairs in Babylon while his father, Nabonidus, the last king of Babylon, spent extensive periods of time at Tema in Arabia. The events of this chapter took place in 539 B.C., the year of Babylon's fall to the Persians, forty-two years after the death of Nebuchadnezzar in 563 B.C."[2]

2. What is the significance of the particular details given in verses 2-4?

_____

_____

_____

_____

The gold and silver goblets . . . taken from the temple in Jerusalem (5:2). Recall Daniel 1:2; see also 2 Kings 24:13; 2 Chronicles 36:7,10; Jeremiah 27:18-22. "Until this time [in Daniel 5], the vessels from the temple in Jerusalem, which had been taken almost seventy years before, had been kept as sacred in the temple treasury of Marduk."[3]

Nebuchadnezzar his father (5:2). "The immediate father of Belshazzar was Nabonidus, not Nebuchadnezzar. It is not unusual for the terms 'father' (verses 11,13,18) and 'son' (verse 22) to be used as equivalents for 'ancestor' and 'descendant.'"[4]

3. Summarize in your own words what happens in verses 5-9.

_____

_____

_____

_____

Third highest ruler in the kingdom (5:7). This title "may refer to being next highest to King Nabonidus and the co-regent Belshazzar, or may be a more general term for a high official."[5]

4. In verses 10-12, what do the queen's words reveal about Daniel's reputation?

_____

_____

_____

_____

For Thought and Discussion: Imagine yourself as one of the guests at Belshazzar's banquet on this occasion described in Daniel 5. As these events unfolded, what would be your prevailing thoughts and feelings?

The queen (5:10). This "most likely refers to the queen mother, since the wives of the king were already present (verse 2)."[6] "This queen is most likely to have been the wife of Nabonidus and mother of Belshazzar."[7] The queen mother was "one of very few women to have significant power in ancient royal courts."[8]

Belteshazzar (5:12). "Daniel's Babylonian name, Belteshazzar, probably means 'O Lady (wife of the god Bel), protect the king!' It is similar to Belshazzar, which means, 'O Bel, protect the king!'"[9]

5. Imagine yourself as Daniel being brought into the scene as described in verses 13-16. What would you consider to be the most important details in the information provided to you here?

_____

_____

_____

6. In verse 17, what does Daniel promise, and on what terms?

For Further Study:
How is Daniel's situation here a later fulfillment of the psalmist's envisioned situation in Psalm 119:46-47? And how is Belshazzar's situation a reflection of Isaiah 26:10?

_____
_____
_____
_____

"Daniel's blunt response [in verse 17] omitted the usual deferential politeness of the Babylonian court."[10]

7. In verses 18-21, what major points does Daniel make to the king?

_____
_____
_____
_____

8. What specific charges does Daniel bring against Belshazzar in verses 22-23 before giving his interpretation of the writing on the wall?

_____
_____
_____
_____

Though you knew all this (5:22). "Because the king is without excuse, even more than his father, the time of mercy is past."[11]

9. Look again at Daniel's comments in verses 18-23. Why do you think he said these particular things in this particular moment?

_____
_____

_____

_____

"Belshazzar knew Babylonian history, and so he knew how God had humbled Nebuchadnezzar. Nevertheless, his banquet was a rebellious challenge to God's authority as he took the sacred vessels from God's temple and drank from them. No one who understands that God is the Creator of the universe would be foolish enough to challenge him."[12]

Optional Application: Each of us shares with King Belshazzar certain truths he was told in the last sentence in Daniel 5:23: God holds in His hand our life and all our ways, and for this He is to be honored. Because God holds *your* life and all *your* ways in His hand, how can you best honor Him at this time?

10. How would you represent in your own words the interpretation of the handwriting as given by Daniel in verses 24-28?

_____

_____

_____

_____

_____

MENE, TEKEL, PARSIN (5:25-28). "The words are clearly Aramaic and form a sequence of weights, decreasing from a mina, to a shekel (1/60th of a mina), to a half-shekel. It was not that the king and wise men could not read them, but they failed to understand their significance for Belshazzar. Read as verbs (with different vowels attached to the Aramaic consonants), the sequence becomes: 'Numbered, numbered, weighted, and divided.'"[13]

Weighed on the scales (5:27). "Measured in the light of God's standards (see Job 31:6; Psalm 62:9; Proverbs 24:12)."[14]

"The writing on the wall is God's answer to the arrogant challenge presented by Belshazzar's pride and his defiance of the God who had shown His existence and sovereignty in the time of Nebuchadnezzar."[15]

11. In verse 29, how would you characterize the king's response to Daniel's words?

_____

_____

_____

_____

12. What quickly happens next, according to verses 30-31?

_____

_____

_____

_____

Belshazzar, king of the Babylonians, was slain (5:30). "It is not known just how Belshazzar died. However, the Greek historians Herodotus and Xenophon report that Babylon was taken in a surprise attack by the Persians while the Babylonians were engaged in reveling and dancing."[16]

Darius the Mede (5:31). "The identity of Darius the Mede and the exact nature of his relationship to Cyrus is not certain. It is clear that Cyrus was already king of Persia at the time when Babylon fell to the Persians (539 B.C.). . . . Some commentators argue that Darius was a Babylonian throne name adopted by Cyrus himself. On this view, 6:28 should be understood as, 'during the reign of Darius the Mede, *that is*, the reign of

Cyrus the Persian.' Others suggest that Darius was actually Cyrus's general, elsewhere named Gubaru or Ugbaru, and credited in the Nabonidus Chronicle with the capture of Babylon."[17] Years later, "there was a Darius on the Persian throne from 522 to 486, Darius I Hystaspes" [the "Darius" mentioned in the books of Ezra, Haggai, and Zechariah]; meanwhile, the ruler mentioned in Daniel 5:31 "is called Darius the Mede perhaps to distinguish him from Darius Hystaspes."[18] Note the further information given about him in Daniel 6 and in 9:1. "The Book of Daniel gives far more information concerning the personal background of Darius the Mede than of Belshazzar or even of Nebuchadnezzar. For he is the only monarch in the book whose age [5:31], parentage [9:1], and nationality [5:31; 9:1] are recorded."[19]

Optional Application: What aspects of Daniel's character, as shown in this chapter, do you believe are strengths that God, by His grace, wants to further develop in your life? How is God already working on this in your life, and how does He want you to respond to His training?

13. For readers of the book of Daniel, how does this chapter further reinforce the lessons conveyed by King Nebuchadnezzar in chapter 4?

_____

_____

_____

_____

14. What most impresses you in this chapter about Daniel's understanding of God?

_____

_____

_____

_____

15. In Daniel 5, what would you select as the key verse or passage — one that best captures or reflects the dynamics of what this chapter is all about?

_____

_____

_____

_____

16. List any lingering questions you have about
Daniel 5.

_____

_____

_____

_____

For the Group

You may want to focus your discussion for lesson 5
especially on the following issues, themes, and concepts. (These will likely reflect what group members
have learned in their individual study of this week's
passage, although they'll also have made discoveries in other areas as well.)

- Our dependence on God
- God's sovereignty over all things
- True heroism
- Godliness
- Pride and humility
- Wisdom
- God's glory

The following numbered questions in lesson 5
may stimulate your best and most helpful discussion: 4, 5, 7, 8, 10, 14, 15, and 16.

Remember to look also at the "For Thought and
Discussion" questions in the margin.

1. Leland Ryken and Philip Graham Ryken, eds., *The Literary
   Study Bible* (Wheaton, IL: Crossway, 2007), at Daniel 5.
2. *New Geneva Study Bible* (Nashville: Thomas Nelson, 1995),
   at Daniel 5:1.
3. *The Complete Word Study Old Testament*, ed. Warren
   Baker (Chattanooga, TN: AMG Publishers, 1994), at Daniel
   5:1-2.
4. *New Geneva*, at Daniel 5:2.
5. *ESV Study Bible* (Wheaton, IL: Crossway, 2008), at Daniel
   5:5-9.

6. *ESV*, at Daniel 5:10.
7. Joyce G. Baldwin, *Daniel: An Introduction and Commentary*, vol. 25, Tyndale Old Testament Commentary (Downers Grove, IL: InterVarsity, 1978), 135.
8. *New Geneva*, at Daniel 5:10.
9. *ESV*, at Daniel 5:12.
10. *ESV*, at Daniel 5:17.
11. *New Geneva*, at Daniel 5:22.
12. *Life Application Bible*, various editions (Wheaton, IL: Tyndale, 1988 and later), at Daniel 5:21-23.
13. *ESV*, at Daniel 5:25.
14. *NIV Study Bible* (Grand Rapids, MI: Zondervan, 1985), at Daniel 5:27.
15. *New Geneva*, at Daniel 5:24.
16. *New Geneva*, at Daniel 5:30.
17. *ESV*, at Daniel 5:30-31.
18. Baldwin, 27.
19. J. C. Whitcomb, in Baldwin, 27–28.

DANIEL 6

In the Lions' Den

"Chapter 6 is perhaps the most striking event in Daniel's life. . . . The specifics belong to an ancient world, but the principles involved are as close as our daily experience."[1]

For Thought and Discussion: The story of Daniel in the lions' den is well known. In the past, what have been your strongest impressions of this episode?

1. How would you characterize Daniel's current situation, as described in verses 1-3?

   _____

   _____

   _____

   _____

By his exceptional qualities (6:3). Or, more literally, "because an excellent spirit was in him" (ESV, NKJV); "he possessed an extraordinary spirit" (NASB). Recall 4:8 and 5:11-12.

2. How does persecution of Daniel develop, according to verses 4-5?

   _____

   _____

59

For Thought and Discussion: The king's officials in Daniel 6 are determined to entrap Daniel, an innocent and honorable man. What are the forces at work in human nature that trigger this kind of animosity?

_____

_____

Tried to find grounds for charges against Daniel (6:4). "Daniel's faithfulness earned him some powerful enemies, either through jealousy or because his incorruptibility restricted their opportunities to enhance their income."[2]

With the law of his God (6:5). "Unintentionally, Daniel's adversaries affirm not only his moral integrity but also the visible nature of his piety and commitment to the God of Israel."[3]

3. In the unfolding plot against Daniel, what transpires in verses 6-9?

_____

_____

_____

The decree that anyone who prays to any god or human being . . . except to you, Your Majesty (6:7). "The proposal would appear to Darius to be more political than religious, and would serve to consolidate his authority over newly conquered territories."[4]

The law of the Medes and Persians, which cannot be repealed (6:8). "The concept of the king's word as inflexible and unchanging law underlined the fixed nature of the king's decisions. While it was always possible for the king to issue a contrary counter-edict, to do so would result in an enormous loss of face."[5] See also Esther 1:19; 8:8.

4. In verse 10, how would you explain Daniel's response?

_____

_____

_____

_____

"Daniel made no attempt to hide his daily prayer routine from his enemies in government, even though he knew this would be disobeying the new law. Hiding his daily prayers would have been futile since the officials surely would have caught him at something else. . . . Also, hiding would have demonstrated that he was afraid of the officials. Daniel continued to pray because he could not look to the king for the guidance and strength that he needed during this difficult time. Only God could provide what he really needed."[6]

On his knees (6:10). "Standing may have been a regular posture in prayer (1 Chronicles 23:30; Nehemiah 9:2-5), while kneeling, a mark of humility, occurred in circumstances of particular solemnity (1 Kings 8:54; Ezra 9:5; Psalm 95:6; Luke 22:41; Acts 7:60; 9:40)."[7]

Three times a day . . . just as he had done before (6:10). "This practice must have made it easy for the satraps and officials to gather the evidence necessary to convict Daniel."[8]

5. What do Daniel's opponents learn about him in verse 11?

_____

_____

For Further Study:
How does Daniel's
praying in this chap-
ter conform to the
earlier patterns given
in these passages:
2 Chronicles 6:38-39;
Psalm 5:7; 55:17; 86:3;
95:6?

_____

_____

6. In verses 12-15, how would you summarize
the next steps of action taken by Daniel's
opponents?

_____

_____

_____

_____

7. What is particularly important about the king's
response to these things as you observe it devel-
oping in verses 12, 14, and 16?

_____

_____

_____

_____

Greatly distressed (6:14). "Darius immediately
perceived that he had been victimized by
the intrigue of his own officials in order to
trap Daniel. His loyalty to Daniel remained
unshaken."[9]

8. Summarize the king's further actions as given
in verses 16-18 and state their significance.

_____

_____

_____

_____

9. Based on verses 19-20, summarize the king's
further actions and indicate their significance.

_____

_____

_____

_____

In the morning, "Darius arose and hurried to the lions' den, where he discovered that Daniel had spent a far more comfortable night surrounded by wild animals than Darius did in his royal luxury."[10]

10. What do you find most significant in Daniel's reply to the king in verses 21-22?

_____

_____

_____

_____

My God sent his angel. . . . I was found innocent in his sight (6:22). "The meaning of Daniel's name, 'God is my judge,' was thus affirmed."[11]

11. Summarize the king's response to Daniel's deliverance as seen in verses 23-24.

_____

_____

_____

_____

The king . . . gave orders to lift Daniel out (6:23). "Darius could rescue Daniel without violating the decree since its demands had been fulfilled."[12]

At the king's command, the men who had falsely accused Daniel were brought in and thrown into the lions' den, along with their wives and children (6:24). "This was in accord with the common principle in the ancient Near East that anyone who made a false charge against someone else should be punished by receiving the same fate they had sought for their victim (see Deuteronomy 19:16-21). In line with the ruthless practice of the Persians, the sentence was also carried out on the families of the guilty men."[13]

Optional Application: Reflect again on Daniel's faith as evidenced and affirmed in this chapter. What are your own best opportunities for demonstrating this same kind of faith?

12. In the king's proclamation in verses 25-27, what does he command and why?

_____

_____

_____

_____

13. How do the words of King Darius in verses 25-27 compare with the words spoken earlier by King Nebuchadnezzar in 4:1-3 and 4:34-35?

_____

_____

_____

"The decree [in 6:26-27] is an eloquent testimony to 'the living God' and His indestructible kingdom. It is an official acknowledgment of Daniel's God, although it does not necessarily reflect personal faith on the part of Darius."[14]

14. What do we learn about Daniel in verse 28?

_____

_____

_____

_____

"This closing comment . . . reminds the reader that Daniel's entire life was spent in exile, in a metaphorical lions' den. Yet God preserved him alive and unharmed throughout the whole of that time, enabling him to prosper under successive kings until the time of King Cyrus, when his prayers for Jerusalem finally began to be answered. Cyrus was God's chosen instrument to bring about the return from the exile, when he issued a decree that the Jews could return to their homeland and rebuild Jerusalem (see 2 Chronicles 36:22-23; Ezra 1:1-3)."[15]

Optional Application: What aspects of Daniel's character, as shown in this chapter, do you believe are strengths that God, by His grace, wants to further develop in your life? How is God already working on this in your life, and how does He want you to respond to His training?

15. What most impresses you in this chapter about Daniel's understanding of God?

_____

_____

_____

_____

16. In Daniel 6, what would you select as the key verse or passage—one that best captures or reflects the dynamics of what this chapter is all about?

_____

_____

_____

_____

DANIEL 9

Daniel's Prayer

"Chapter 9 takes on special significance. ... What an individual is in secret, on his knees before God, that he is and no more. Since this is so, it is in this chapter that we learn who Daniel really was and discover the secret of his usefulness in God's kingdom. He was a man of prayer."[1]

1. Chapter 9 has been called the key to the book of Daniel. Why might this be so?

   _____

   _____

   _____

   _____

2. What is the important background to Daniel's prayer in this chapter (see verses 1-2)?

   _____

   _____

   _____

   _____

In the first year (9:1). "The first year of the Persian empire, 539 B.C., and referred to in Ezra 1:1 as the first year of Cyrus king of Persia."[2]

Darius son of Xerxes (a Mede by descent) (9:1). "The king already named in 5:31 and chapter 6. . . . If the identity of Darius and Cyrus as one and the same person be accepted . . . this ruler was able to claim descent from both Median and Persian ancestors. The two nations were closely related, and such an ancestry would commend him to both."[3]

Seventy years (9:2). See Jeremiah 25:11. "The interval between the first deportation in 605 B.C., in which Daniel himself was involved [recall Daniel 1:1-6], and 536 B.C., when the first returnees under Zerubbabel once more set up an altar in Jerusalem [see Ezra 3:1-2] amounted to seventy years. Likewise, the interval between the destruction of the first temple by Nebuzaradan in 586 [see 2 Kings 25:9] and the completion of the second temple by Zerubbabel in 516 [see Ezra 6:14-15] was about seventy years."[4] "There are various ways of reckoning the years of exile, none of which comes exactly to seventy years; but theologically the important point was that restoration marked acceptance with the Lord, who, by restoring his people to their land, demonstrated that he had forgiven and reinstated them. It is possible to be so preoccupied with numbers as to miss the essential truth which those numbers declare."[5]

3. a. In verses 3-10, what do you find significant in Daniel's manner of praying?

_____

_____

_____

 b. What does Daniel demonstrate concerning his true understanding of God?

_____

_____

_____

_____

c. What does Daniel demonstrate concerning his understanding of God's people?

_____

_____

_____

Pleaded . . . in prayer and petition (9:3). "Divine decree or no, the Scriptures never support the idea that God's purpose will be accomplished irrespective of the prayers of his people. Daniel, by taking God at his word and expecting him to honor it, was rewarded not only by an assurance that his prayer was heard (9:23) but also by a further revelation (9:24-27)."[6] "The restoration did take place, not only as the fulfillment of prophecy, but also in answer to the cries of God's people. Daniel, a man of prayer, wanted God's people to see the intimate connection between their praying and the events of history."[7]

"We miss the point of the constant emphasis on Daniel's understanding, wisdom, and discernment (see 1:17,20; 5:11-12; 9:22; 10:1) if we fail to see that it led him to become a man of prayer. Yet this is constantly reiterated throughout the book. His recognition of his own role, his discernment of the weakness of the people and the opposition they faced all drove him to commune with God."[8]

Lord, you are righteous (9:7). See also 9:16. "In Scripture, 'righteousness' basically means

In his prayer in verse 11, Daniel makes mention of the consequences of Israel's disobedience. According to Leviticus 26:14-45 and Deuteronomy 28:15-68, how did God make these plain beforehand?

For Thought and Discussion: We've seen earlier, in Daniel 6:10, that Daniel did not try to conceal his prayer life. Imagine yourself in the background as you observe Daniel in the prayerful situation described in 9:3. What conclusions and impressions concerning this man Daniel would likely be present in your mind?

'integrity.' Sometimes it is defined as 'conformity to a norm.' In the case of God, the norm to which He conforms is His own being and character. He is true to Himself; He always acts in character."[9]

Merciful and forgiving (9:9). "The prayer is so worded that the deadlock created by Israel's rebellion may be broken. Only if the Lord's mercy and forgiveness prevail can the relationship be restored between him and his people. . . . The lengths to which God would go to make reconciliation possible (Romans 3:21-26) were not yet revealed."[10]

4. How does Daniel view his country's recent history, according to the words of his prayer in verses 11-14?

_____

_____

_____

5. a. Reflect on the words of Daniel's prayer in verses 14-15. What does he further acknowledge about God?

_____

_____

_____

b. What does he acknowledge again concerning God's people?

_____

_____

_____

c. Why are these confessions important in this particular prayer at this particular time?

_____

_____

6. What are the specific requests Daniel makes in verses 16-19, and why are they important?

_____

_____

_____

_____

For your sake, my God (9:19). "Daniel's ultimate motive for prayer was the glory of God because it was his great motive for living."[11]

7. From all you've seen throughout Daniel's prayer, what is the actual *basis* for the requests he finally makes in verses 16-19?

_____

_____

_____

_____

8. What is significant in the way Daniel summarizes his prayer in verse 20?

_____

_____

_____

_____

9. What do you find most significant in God's encouraging response to Daniel's prayer (see verses 21-23)?

_____

_____

For Further Study: What important connections do you see between Daniel's prayer in Daniel 9:1-20 and the prayer of King Solomon, centuries earlier, as recorded in 1 Kings 8:46-53 (also in 2 Chronicles 6:36-40)?

For Further Study: What connections and commonalities do you see between the long prayers recorded in Ezra 9, Nehemiah 9, and Daniel 9?

Optional Application: What aspects of Daniel's prayer in chapter 9 are most important to you in serving as a model for your praying in the future?

_____

_____

_____

_____

The time of the evening sacrifice (9:21). "It had
   been many decades since Daniel had been in
   Jerusalem where the evening offering was
   made (roughly midafternoon). Yet his thinking
   was still regulated by the life and worship of
   Jerusalem."[12]

Highly esteemed (9:23). Or, "greatly loved" (ESV);
   "greatly beloved" (NKJV). "Daniel was loved in
   heaven because he lived for God."[13] The Hebrew
   term means "literally 'precious things' or 'a
   precious treasure.' . . . God had taken pleasure
   in this intercessor because his heart was wholly
   set on the will and glory of the Lord. His faith
   was precious in God's eyes."[14]

Consider the word (9:23). "It requires study. . . .
   Wisdom and understanding were a gift (verse
   22), but he was still told to consider the word
   and understand the vision."[15] Compare 10:11.

Understand the vision (9:23). "What was there for
   Daniel to understand? Presumably he needed
   help in understanding verses 24-27. While
   Gabriel's greeting is enigmatic, it provides a
   major clue to this section. The reason for his
   appearance at that time was the way in which
   Daniel's prayer had focused on the end of the
   seventy-year period prophesied by Jeremiah.
   The Lord wanted His faithful servant to see
   those seventy years in a new and sharper
   focus."[16]

---

10. What are the major points Gabriel makes in his
   words to Daniel in verse 24?

_____

_____

_____

Verse 24 explains that at the end of the "seventy 'sevens,'" "six goals will have been accomplished.... These are the ends to which God is working....

"The six verbs divide into two sets of three; the first three are concerned with the problem which exercised Daniel in his prayer, namely the grounds on which God could forgive human sin, and the second three with the positive fulfillment of God's right purposes."[17]

"It is almost instinctive to the New Testament Christian to see in these statements a prophecy of the work of Christ."[18]

Seventy "sevens" (9:24). Or "seventy weeks" (ESV, NASB, NKJV).

"Most interpreters view the units of 'seventy weeks' as representing 490 years.... Interpretations differ over whether these subunits are to be viewed as a continuous sequence or as having time intervals between them."[19]

"There are many suggested interpretations of the 'seventy weeks' (or 'seventy sevens'), but there are three main views: (1) the passage refers to events surrounding Antiochus IV Epiphanes (175–164 B.C.); (2) the 70 sevens are to be understood figuratively; and (3) the passage refers to events around the time of Christ.... The important point is that God has appointed the amount of time, and thus his people should not lose heart."[20]

Those who view the 490 years as relating to the time of Christ "may be divided into two groups: (a) those who interpret the passage as having its primary focus on events associated with the first advent of Christ and

(continued on page 102)

For Further Study:
Reflect further on the six things that will take place at the end of the "seventy 'sevens'" or "seventy weeks" mentioned in Daniel 9:24. Describe how you see these specific things connected to the work of Christ in these passages: Matthew 1:21; Luke 1:35; 4:18-21; 24:25-27,44-45; John 3:34; Acts 3:19-21; Romans 3:21-22; 5:10; 1 Corinthians 1:30; 2 Corinthians 5:18-21; Philippians 3:9; Colossians 1:20; 2:14; Hebrews 1:8-9; 2:17; 7:26; 9:26; 10:14; 1 John 3:8.

(continued from page 101)

shortly thereafter; (b) those who interpret the passage as having reference to events associated with both the first and second advents of Christ with an unstated time interval between the two. Within each of these categories, individual interpreters differ on details."[21]

"There are many difficulties in deciding between these interpretations, which also involve questions of the proper approach to interpreting biblical prophecy. In all of this it is crucial not to miss Daniel's message for his audience, namely, that God has allotted the amount of time for these events, and therefore his people should trust and endure."[22]

From Daniel's perspective, "the first coming of Christ is the focal point of the forward look, though the second coming in judgment is also envisaged. To him the seventy years covered the whole of future time, and the coming of the kingdom looked from his vantage-point like one event. It is in the light of the New Testament that we have learnt to separate the first and second comings of Christ, and with the help of his teaching to realize that there is a recognizable pattern in history which his followers do well to note and expect to see worked out in the events of their own lifetime."[23]

11. What further specific details does Gabriel give in verses 25-27?

_____

_____

_____

_____

Rebuilt (9:25). "This is clear and genuine encouragement for Daniel. He longs for the restoration of Jerusalem and is told that it will be rebuilt despite considerable opposition and difficulty (as the Book of Nehemiah bears witness)."[24]

An abomination that causes desolation (9:27).
See Matthew 24:15.

"Interpreters do not agree on how to handle Gabriel's vision of the future (verses 24-27), but whatever historical references the vision might contain, we will not go wrong if we give the vision an eschatological, end-times interpretation."[25]

"The New Testament nowhere clearly refers to the contents of this prophecy. Even the reference to 'the abomination of desolation' in Mark 13:14 is from Daniel 11:31 and 12:11 and not strictly from 9:27. If the seventy weeks of this prophecy were *fundamental* to a biblical theology, there would undoubtedly be clear exposition of the passage in the apostolic writings."[26]

12. What do you think would be God's purpose in revealing to Daniel the things Gabriel speaks of in verses 25-27?

_____

_____

_____

_____

"Each verse in 24-27 is set in the same overall time frame of seventy sevens:
   "Verse 24 covers the entire period;
   "Verse 25 divides the first sixty-nine sevens;
   "Verse 26 describes the final seven in indefinite terms;

(continued on page 104)

For Further Study:
What connections do you see between the prophecies given in Daniel 9:26-27 and the words of Jesus in Matthew 24:15-28?

Optional Application: What aspects of Daniel's character, as shown especially in his prayer in this chapter, do you believe are strengths that God, by His grace, wants to further develop in your life? How is God already working on this in your life, and how does He want you to respond to His training?

(continued from page 103)

"Verse 27 describes the final seven in more detail.

"If this understanding of the structure is correct, then the first half of verse 27 refers to Christ, the second half to the destruction of the city and the abominations involved in its downfall at the hands of Titus Flavius Vespasianus in A.D. 70. In the middle of the final week Christ died for His people. He brought all sacrifice to an end (as the Letter to the Hebrews underlines). Within four decades from the Messiah's rejection, the soil on which the temple was built, so beloved by Daniel, would once again be defiled by pagans. Jerusalem would again be desolate.

"If this is the correct interpretation, it is not too difficult to see what it was that heaven was so anxious to communicate to Daniel, its representative on earth. It was right that he should long to see the people delivered from captivity; it was right that he should long to see Jerusalem rebuilt and the temple worship reinstituted. Yet the Lord wanted Daniel to see beyond these things to what they foreshadowed, however painful that might be.

"God's ultimate purpose was not a temple made with hands and a holy place entered but once each year. His Son was the place in which men were to approach God; His sacrifice was the one which would bring forgiveness. Then if men still clung to the shadows and symbols of the old order, rejecting what they symbolized, there was only one terrible prospect: judgment and destruction of the most terrible kind."[27]

***

The Anointed One will be put to death and will have nothing (9:26). Or, "Messiah shall be cut off, but not for Himself" (NKJV). "This verb (*kārat*) is used of 'cutting a covenant,' a ritual which involved the death of the sacrificial victim (Genesis 15:10,18); it was also frequently used of death generally."[28]

An abomination that causes desolation (9:27). See also 8:13; 11:31; 12:11.

13. What most impresses you in this chapter about Daniel's understanding of God?

_____

_____

_____

_____

14. In Daniel 9, what would you select as the key verse or passage—one that best captures or reflects the dynamics of what this chapter is all about?

_____

_____

_____

_____

15. List any lingering questions you have about Daniel 9.

_____

_____

_____

_____

For the Group

You may want to focus your discussion for lesson 9 especially on the following issues, themes, and concepts. (These will likely reflect what group members have learned in their individual study of this week's passage, although they'll also have made discoveries in other areas as well.)

- Our dependence on God
- God's sovereignty over all things
- True heroism
- Godliness
- Perseverance
- Prayer

- God's faithfulness
- Wisdom and understanding
- Future history and the end of this world

   The following numbered questions in lesson 9 may stimulate your best and most helpful discussion: 3, 5, 6, 7, 9, 12, 13, 14, and 15.
   Remember to look also at the "For Thought and Discussion" questions in the margin.

1. Sinclair Ferguson, *Daniel*, The Preacher's Commentary, ed. Lloyd J. Ogilvie (Nashville: Thomas Nelson, 1988), 171–172.
2. Joyce G. Baldwin, *Daniel: An Introduction and Commentary*, vol. 25, Tyndale Old Testament Commentary (Downers Grove, IL: InterVarsity, 1978), 182.
3. Baldwin, 182–183.
4. Gleason L. Archer Jr., *Daniel*, vol. 7, Expositor's Bible Commentary, ed. Frank E. Gaebelein (Grand Rapids, MI: Zondervan, 1985), 31.
5. Baldwin, 183.
6. Baldwin, 184.
7. Ferguson, 174.
8. Ferguson, 192.
9. Ferguson, 178.
10. Ferguson, 185.
11. Ferguson, 179.
12. Ferguson, 183.
13. Ferguson, 184.
14. Archer, 112.
15. Baldwin, 186–187.
16. Ferguson, 183.
17. Baldwin, 187.
18. Ferguson, 186.
19. *New Geneva Study Bible* (Nashville: Thomas Nelson, 1995), at Daniel 9:24.
20. *ESV Study Bible* (Wheaton, IL: Crossway, 2008), at Daniel 9:24-27.
21. *New Geneva*, at Daniel 9:24-27.
22. *ESV*, at Daniel 9:24-27.
23. Baldwin, 197.
24. Ferguson, 187.
25. Leland Ryken and Philip Graham Ryken, eds., *The Literary Study Bible* (Wheaton, IL: Crossway, 2007), at Daniel 9.
26. Ferguson, 182.
27. Ferguson, 187–188.
28. Baldwin, 190.

DANIEL 10

A Heavenly Conflict

In the final three chapters of Daniel, we behold
"a final vision concerning the future reign of
Antiochus IV Epiphanes, but looking beyond his
reign to another that culminates at the end of the
age."[1] "Conflicts on earth reflect conflicts in the
heavens, and this will continue to the end, when
God will ultimately triumph."[2] "As Daniel ascended
the hill of God's revelation and was brought nearer
to the crisis points in that conflict, he inevitably
found those peaks merging into each other, sometimes (to him at least and at times also to us)
indistinguishably. It is not always easy for us to
determine where the vision of an intermediate
conflict merges into a vision of the last and greatest
conflict."[3]

"Chapter 10 contains vital biblical insights
into the nature of reality. It emphasizes
that human causes and effects are not
the only forces or influences operative
in the history of the world. . . . Here in
chapter 10 God tells Daniel something
new and important which (rightly
understood) will enable him (and us) to
have peace and be strong."[4]

For Thought and Discussion: As you observe what Daniel does in 10:2-3, how appropriate do you think such actions would be for believers today? What would justify this kind of behavior from us?

For Further Study: Reflect again on the prayerful Daniel we see in 10:2-3. Describe how this picture compares with what you see in these passages: 1 Samuel 7:5-9; 2 Samuel 12:16-17; 2 Chronicles 20:3-4; Ezra 8:21-23; 9:4-5; Nehemiah 1:4; 9:1; Esther 4:3; Psalm 35:13-14; 69:9-11; 109:22-24; Isaiah 37:1; Joel 2:12-17; Jonah 3:5-9; Acts 13:2-3. (Explore the contexts of these verses to further understand each situation.)

1. What important details regarding Daniel's next vision are given in verse 1?

_____

_____

_____

_____

In the third year of Cyrus (10:1). "The third year after his conquest of Babylonia in 539 B.C.,"[5] that is, 536 B.C. "Two years earlier, the first party of Jewish exiles had returned to Jerusalem in response to Cyrus's decree, but they faced severe opposition and by this point had ceased their rebuilding work."[6] See Ezra 1–4.

"What is so remarkable about Daniel here is the way in which he consecrated himself to the advance of God's kingdom, even though he was not directly involved in the rebuilding of the temple, nor would he live to see it. That is the hallmark of true faith and commitment. He believed but did not receive what was promised (see Hebrews 11:33). He prayed for blessing he would never personally witness."[7]

2. What further background information to this vision does Daniel provide in verses 2-4?

_____

_____

_____

_____

3. In verses 5-6, what are the most prominent features of the man whom Daniel now sees in his vision?

_____

_____

_____

"There is much to be said for seeing this revelation as a Christophany [an appearance of the preincarnate Christ].

"The description of this figure and the impact of his presence on Daniel and the others far surpasses anything that is said of either Gabriel or Michael. Furthermore, there are similarities between this vision and other biblical theophanies or Christophanies (for example, Ezekiel 1:26ff. and especially Revelation 1:12-15, where Christ is described in somewhat similar terms as He walks among the churches). Additionally, Daniel addresses the figure in terms of reverence not found in his conversations with the others. He calls him 'my Lord' three times (verses 16,17,19). . . .

"More important than identifying the figure . . . is recognizing the impression the vision is intended to create. Even if the figure is not divine, Daniel's vision . . . communicated to him a sense of the omnipotence and all-gloriousness of God. It reveals His absolute sufficiency to meet the needs of His people."[8]

Another view: "This glorious figure was unable to complete his task without the help of Michael, one of the chief princes (verse 13), so it is unlikely that this is a physical manifestation of God or Christ. More probably, he is one of the angelic attendants of God, who reflect their master's glory (see Ezekiel 1; 10). The revelation of God's glory shining through

For Further Study:
How would you
compare the descrip-
tion of the mes-
senger in Daniel
10:5-6 with the way
Jesus is described in
Revelation 1:10-16?
What are the similari-
ties and differences?

this mighty creature was overwhelming,
crushing Daniel to the ground and send-
ing his companions scurrying for cover."⁹

Dressed in linen (10:5). "Linen garments were
worn by the priests. In particular, the high
priest wore linen when he went into the holy
place (Exodus 28:42; Leviticus 6:10; 16:4). This
would have reminded the exiled Daniel of the
temple sacrifices and the Day of Atonement,
the way of forgiveness ordained by God."¹⁰

Like lightning (10:6). "Lightning is a frequent
accompaniment to the coming of the Lord in
Scripture (compare Ezekiel 1:13-14; Revelation
4:5; 8:5; 11:19; 16:18) and was so supremely at
Sinai (Exodus 19:16; 20:18)."¹¹

His voice like the sound of a multitude (10:6).
"Perhaps not only in its strength but also in its
richness of tone."¹²

4. From the description in verse 7, how would you
explain what happens here?

_____

_____

_____

_____

I, Daniel, . . . the only one (10:7). "I, Daniel,
alone" (ESV, NASB, NKJV). "Throughout the book
he is obviously a man apart. Now he is a man
alone, but the truth of the matter was that he
was never less alone in all his life."¹³

Those who were with me did not see it (10:7).
This is somewhat similar to the experiences of
the companions of Saul (Paul) on the road to
Damascus, as Paul testifies in Acts 22:9.

5. Summarize Daniel's response as described in verse 8.

_____

_____

_____

_____

6. Express in your own words what Daniel experiences and hears in verses 9-11.

_____

_____

_____

_____

Highly esteemed (10:11). "Literally reads, 'man of preciousness' (compare 9:23). This remarkable greeting reassured Daniel of the personal love and concern that the Almighty has for each one of his faithful servants. . . . Observe that Daniel's privileged status as one especially precious to God resulted from his complete absorption in the will and glory of the Lord to whom he had yielded his heart. His was the whole-souled devotion of a Paul or a Moses."[14]

7. What does verse 12 reveal about Daniel and about God?

_____

_____

_____

_____

For Further Study:
What more do you
learn about Michael
in Jude 1:9 and
Revelation 12:7-8?
(Some consider that
Michael may also be
the angel mentioned
in Revelation 20:1 and
the "one who now
holds" the man of sin
in 2 Thessalonians
2:6-7.)

Your words were heard, and I have come in
   response to them (10:12). "The vision and
   revelation that Daniel received came as a direct
   response to his prayers."[15]

8. What significance do you see in the background
   information given in verse 13?

   _____

   _____

   _____

   _____

The prince of the Persian kingdom (10:13).
   "Apparently a demon exercising influence over
   the Persian realm in the interests of Satan (see
   also verse 20)."[16]

Michael, one of the chief princes (10:13). "Michael
   appears to have a special responsibility to care
   for the nation of Israel (see verse 21; 12:1)."[17]

Resisted me. . . . I was detained (10:13). "Here
   is a glimpse of spiritual battles waged in
   'heavenly places' and affecting events on earth
   (see Ephesians 6:12; Revelation 12:7-9). The
   power of fallen angels is limited by God, as is
   made clear here and elsewhere in Scripture
   (Job 1:12; 2:6)."[18]

9. In verse 14, this messenger states his purpose
   in coming to Daniel. Why is this important?

   _____

   _____

   _____

   _____

10. Summarize Daniel's further response as seen in
    verses 15-17.

_____
_____
_____
_____

Speechless (10:15). "He was literally deprived of
the power of speech until he received a second
supernatural touch, this time on his lips, and
was given power of speech once again."[19]

My strength is gone and I can hardly breathe
(10:17). "When he is thus emptied of all confidence in his own resources, he is strengthened
by grace (verse 18) and given the ability to be
strong (verse 19)."[20]

11. Describe what Daniel goes on to experience as
    narrated in verses 18-19.

_____
_____
_____
_____

12. What is the importance of the details given in
    verses 20-21 of this chapter (and continuing in
    11:1)?

_____
_____
_____
_____

Do you know why I have come to you? (10:20).
This "tantalizing question" addressed to Daniel
"is intended to stimulate him to think over
the message he has received and recognize its
wider implications."[21]

113

**Optional
Application:** Reflect
on Daniel's experi-
ence in 10:17-19 of
finding strength in
the Lord when he
needed it most. What
message here relates
to your own lack of
resources in yourself?
In what ways are
you in need of being
strengthened by the
Lord?

**Optional
Application:** From
your study so far in
the book of Daniel,
what have you
become convinced
of regarding spiritual
warfare? What do you
see as your own part
in this conflict, and
what does it require
from you?

"Daniel's special concern had apparently been to understand the prospects of the people of God during the Medo-Persian kingdom and then during the Greek Empire. The heavenly apostle comes to reveal to him what will take place. Precisely because this will stir up Daniel (and perhaps others) to pray for the kingdom of God, that the gates of hell will not withstand it, opposition is mounted. . . . The conflict envisaged is not one with flesh and blood but against principalities, powers, the spiritual hosts of wickedness in the heavenly places (Ephesians 6:12). This is why Daniel needs to be 'strong in the Lord' (Ephesians 6:10). Nor is this conflict a momentary one. It will be engaged again (Daniel 10:20). It is perpetual."[22]

First I will tell you (10:21). "The vision is intended to give unshakeable assurance that, desperate as the situation will be, God is so fully in control as to be able to disclose the sequence of events before they happen."[23]

Book of Truth (10:21). See also 12:1. This book "most likely refers to the plan that God has for Israel and the world. The conflict against these satanic forces continues to this day, though the human adversary constantly changes."[24]

"The narrative function of this chapter is to serve as a prelude to the ensuing visions of the future."[25]

"Remember that chapters 10, 11, and 12 are a unity."[26]

114

13. Based on all that Daniel sees and experiences in this chapter, what would you say he's learning most about God?

_____

_____

_____

_____

14. In Daniel 10, what would you select as the key verse or passage—one that best captures or reflects the dynamics of what this chapter is all about?

_____

_____

_____

_____

15. List any lingering questions you have about Daniel 10.

_____

_____

_____

_____

For the Group

You may want to focus your discussion for lesson 10 especially on the following issues, themes, and concepts. (These will likely reflect what group members have learned in their individual study of this week's passage, although they'll also have made discoveries in other areas as well.)

- Our dependence on God
- God's sovereignty over all things
- Wisdom and understanding
- Perseverance
- God's faithfulness

- Spiritual conflict
- The nature of evil
- Future history and the end of this world

The following numbered questions in lesson 10 may stimulate your best and most helpful discussion: 3, 7, 9, 13, 14, and 15.

Remember to look also at the "For Thought and Discussion" questions in the margin.

1. *New Geneva Study Bible* (Nashville: Thomas Nelson, 1995), at Daniel 10:1–12:13.
2. *ESV Study Bible* (Wheaton, IL: Crossway, 2008), at Daniel 10:1–12:13.
3. Sinclair Ferguson, *Daniel*, The Preacher's Commentary, ed. Lloyd J. Ogilvie (Nashville: Thomas Nelson, 1988), 205.
4. Ferguson, 189–190.
5. *NIV Study Bible* (Grand Rapids, MI: Zondervan, 1985), at Daniel 10:1.
6. *ESV*, at Daniel 10:1.
7. Ferguson, 192.
8. Ferguson, 194–195.
9. *ESV*, at Daniel 10:5-6.
10. Ferguson, 195.
11. Ferguson, 195.
12. Ferguson, 194.
13. Ferguson, 201.
14. Gleason L. Archer Jr., *Daniel*, vol. 7, Expositor's Bible Commentary, ed. Frank E. Gaebelein (Grand Rapids, MI: Zondervan, 1985), 124.
15. *New Geneva*, at Daniel 10:12.
16. *NIV*, at Daniel 10:13.
17. *ESV*, at Daniel 10:13.
18. *New Geneva*, at Daniel 10:13.
19. Joyce G. Baldwin, *Daniel: An Introduction and Commentary*, vol. 25, Tyndale Old Testament Commentary (Downers Grove, IL: InterVarsity, 1978), 202.
20. Ferguson, 196.
21. Ferguson, 197.
22. Ferguson, 198.
23. Baldwin, 202.
24. *ESV*, at Daniel 10:21.
25. Leland Ryken and Philip Graham Ryken, eds., *The Literary Study Bible* (Wheaton, IL: Crossway, 2007), at Daniel 10.
26. Ferguson, 215.

DANIEL 11

A Vision of Earthly Conflicts

This chapter of Daniel includes details with innumerable links—far more than can be mentioned in this study guide—to events later recorded in history, especially in the second century BC. "Any reader who is not a student of ancient history finds the many allusions baffling."[1] But when our focus is on discovering the patterns of God's larger perspective and purposes related to all of history—and to each of our lives—the study of this chapter proves its true worth. "Prophecy is not history written in advance of the time; rather it is present or future history interpreted from the standpoint of God's Word."[2]

In this chapter, "we are bombarded with a host of details regarding what will happen in the future and that are envisioned in the imagination, since they have not yet happened. The details, moreover, appear in a kaleidoscopic and phantasmagoric pattern, and the effect is that we are reading something in code. . . . If we read at a symbolic level, it is obvious that the main ingredients of the vision—the rise and fall of empires, international warfare, an endless succession of nations

117

and rulers that have their day and then vanish — constitute a pattern that is always in the process of being fulfilled in earthly history."[3]

"In the events which the messenger goes on to foretell, the glorious land, the temple, and the wise among the people are at the center of the writer's concern. Two hundred years of Persian rule are passed over in a verse (11:2) because they are not relevant to his theme; the Greek empire, and the struggles between two eastern areas, have more attention (11:3-20) because armies were to march through Judea and put increasing pressure on God's people.

"All this, however, is merely leading into the main theme, the time of oppression which is to overthrow all that the loyal believer holds dear. Whereas the Exile [to Babylon] had been explained by the prophets and accepted in the end by the people as a judgment well deserved, this coming terror is not presented in those terms. It is rather the brutal attack of a megalomaniac against 'the holy covenant' (11:28)." . . .

Thus the messenger warns that "suffering was not always in the nature of divine punishment, as the Exile had been. Rulers of the nations, in so far as they ignore God and are a law to themselves, become beasts who oppress others. At their hands the godly are to suffer, and the chapter shows how one such tyrant comes to behave as he does."[4]

"Daniel had been praying for the people of God. . . . Now the curtain, beyond which his prayers traveled invisibly, was momentarily lifted, and he realized the drama of heavenly warfare in which his intercession had involved him. No wonder he was awestruck by what he saw."[5]

1. Explain in your own words the most important details that Daniel is told in verses 1-4.

_____

_____

_____

_____

I took my stand to support and protect him (11:1). This verse properly belongs to the close of chapter 10, which describes the angel's alliance with the archangel, Michael, against the demons of Persia and Greece.

2. What are the most important particulars given to Daniel in verses 5-6?

_____

_____

_____

"Although there are inevitable difficulties in [Daniel 11], there is wide agreement among commentators about the general outline of the history to which it points."[7]

3. Summarize the most important elements in the message given to Daniel in verses 7-10.

_____

_____

Optional Application: As with the predictions in Daniel 8, the "selective yet detailed overview of the flow of history" here in Daniel 11 is regarded by "some scholars . . . as a 'prophecy after the fact' that was actually written later than the events in the mid-second century B.C. because of the detail and accuracy of its predictions."[6] But passages such as Isaiah 41:21-27, 44:6-7, 46:8-11, and 48:3-8 review the Lord's forthright assertions of his ability to foretell events. What personally convinces *you* that these prophesied events in the book of Daniel were indeed written "before the fact"? What do your beliefs about this have to say concerning your view of God, and why is this important?

For Thought and Discussion: In the mass of information that Daniel is given in chapter 8, which elements impress you most vividly and powerfully?

_____

_____

4. Continue explaining in your own words the most important details given to Daniel in verses 11-13.

_____

_____

_____

_____

5. In verse 14-16, what further important information does Daniel learn?

_____

_____

_____

6. What is most significant in the details given to Daniel in verses 17-19?

_____

_____

_____

7. Summarize the most important elements in the message given to Daniel in verses 20-24.

_____

_____

_____

8. In verses 25-28, what further important information does Daniel learn?

_____

_____

_____

_____

"There is universal agreement that Antiochus Epiphanes (175–163) fulfilled the description given here [beginning in Daniel 11:21, 'a contemptible person'], but we may well wonder why so much space should be given in Scripture to an obscure (to us) upstart of the second century B.C. Why should he be the subject of a special revelation, and why should the Christian reader concern himself with him? . . .

"What distinguishes Antiochus is that he attempts to unify his kingdom by imposing a particular ideology. Nebuchadnezzar had attempted this on one occasion (Daniel 3); a ruler was coming who would make religion his main tool in imposing his will, and so would precipitate a conflict between commitment to the one God, revealed to his people, and the worldly-wise, unscrupulous way of life advocated by diplomacy. In the unequal struggle, God's faithful servants would go through intense suffering. The era of the persecution of 'the church' had begun.

"Consequently the chapter speaks to generations of believers. . . . Rulers will commit themselves wholly to fulfill their ambitions, regardless of what is right. Antiochus is the prototype of many who will come after him, hence the interest shown here in his methods and progress."[8]

The holy covenant (11:28,30). See also verses 22 and 32 as well as Daniel's prayer in 9:4.

9. Continue explaining in your own words the most important details given here to Daniel in verses 29-32.

_____

_____

For Further Study:
To further explore
the theme of "the
abomination that
causes desolation"
(Daniel 11:31; see
also 8:13; 9:27; 12:11),
summarize what you
discover in these
passages: Matthew
24:15-19; Mark 13:14-
23; Luke 21:20-24;
Revelation 17:4-5;
21:27.

_____

_____

The abomination that causes desolation (11:31).
Recall 8:13 and 9:27. "This refers . . . to an
activity of Antiochus Epiphanes, but that
activity is the embryonic form of an evil
that all antichrists perpetrate in one form or
another. Hence Jesus uses the expression in
Mark 13:14, and further allusions to it appear
in the New Testament's teachings on the last
things."[9]

***Those who forsake the holy covenant . . . those
who have violated the covenant*** (11:30,32).
"Evil cannot gain a foothold in the city of God
unless it finds a spirit of cooperation among
the visible people of God. It is not inevitable
that the church should be corrupted by the
world; there must be a willingness or a blind-
ness in the church before that happens."[10]

In studying Daniel 11, we "must face the
inevitable question: How is such a passage
as this 'profitable for doctrine, for reproof, for
correction, for instruction in righteousness'
(2 Timothy 3:16)? Should we not simply accept
the verdict that this section is valuable only
as an outline of ancient history? The answer
must be 'No.' . . .
    "No right-thinking communicator would
present such material as this merely as a history lesson for one important reason: It is
not history — it is prophecy. It foretells the
future in a remarkable way. Understanding
this should fill our hearts with fresh reverence
for the wonders that are contained in God's
Word."[11]

10. What do you see as most significant in the
    words spoken to Daniel in verses 33-35?

_____

_____

_____

_____

Those who are wise will instruct many (11:33). "This likely refers to those who truly fear God and who will encourage others to fight and even die rather than perform abominations before God. This refers primarily to the Maccabean Revolt [the Jewish rebellion in Palestine against their Seleucid rulers beginning in 167 BC]."[12]

Fall by the sword or be burned or captured or plundered (11:33). These words "sum up the sufferings of faithful men and women to this day. . . . Daniel and his friends had been delivered by unusual divine interventions from death [Daniel 3; 6], but the warning here is that this will not always be the case."[13]

Some of the wise will stumble (11:35). "God's messenger describes a time of trial when even wise believers may stumble. This could mean (1) falling into sin, (2) being fearful and losing faith, (3) mistakenly following wrong teaching, or (4) experiencing severe suffering and martyrdom. If we persevere in our faith, any such experience will only refine us and make us stronger."[14]

Optional Application: Have you recently experienced a time of "stumbling" as spoken of in Daniel 11:35? If so, how is God using this and its aftermath to refine you and strengthen you? How is this experience helping you persevere in your faith?[15]

The wording of verse 36 "points to some period between the days of Antiochus and the last day of history. During that time there will be apostasies and refinings among the visible people of God."[16]

"From [verse 36] to the end of chapter 11, the antichrist is in view. The details of this section do not fit what is known of Antiochus Epiphanes."[17]

123

> "If indeed these verses do refer ultimately to the personification of enmity against God in the figure of the Antichrist, then there will inevitably be many foreshadowings of his character. . . . History is frequently punctuated by those who share his kingdom and whose lifestyles resemble what his will be. No wonder that precursors of the antichrist have been taken to be the final Antichrist (see 1 John 2:18)."[18]

11. Finally, from what you see in verses 36-45, what is most important for us to understand about the king who is described here and the actions he takes?

_____

_____

_____

_____

The beautiful holy mountain (11:45). "Mount Zion, or the city of Jerusalem."[19] See Psalm 48:2; Micah 4:2; Hebrews 12:22.

He will come to his end, and no one will help him (11:45). "His defeat will be as inauspicious as his rise to power was meteoric. There is a devastating — presumably deliberate — anticlimax to the progress of evil. In fact, 'The Lord will consume [him] with the breath of His mouth and destroy with the brightness of his coming' (2 Thessalonians 2:8). Christ will simply blow him away."[20]

12. Go back over this chapter and notice all the places where the simple word *but* is used and the statements that are introduced there. What pattern do you find, and what does it reveal about the effectiveness of worldly rulers in plotting their schemes?

_____

_____

_____

_____

13. What are the strongest parallels you see between what Daniel observes in this chapter and his vision in chapter 8?

_____

_____

_____

_____

14. From what Daniel sees and experiences in this chapter, what would you say he is learning most about God?

_____

_____

_____

_____

15. From what Daniel sees and experiences in this chapter, what would you say are the chief lessons he is learning about the world and its future history?

_____

_____

_____

_____

For Thought and Discussion: If these things Daniel observed in chapter 11 truly represent patterns and dynamics we can expect to see throughout history, relate them to what you know about our most recent centuries of world history. What connections do you see?

"After all is said on this difficult chapter, we should not lose sight of the fact that its whole function was to encourage Daniel to faithfulness in prayer. By showing him that the real conflict lying behind world

125

events is spiritual (in chapter 10), the Lord was teaching Daniel that the real weapon of the church is prayer. Fail in the work of prayer, and we fail to understand this great vision."[21]

16. In Daniel 11, what would you select as the key verse or passage—one that best captures or reflects the dynamics of what this chapter is all about?

_____

_____

_____

_____

17. List any lingering questions you have about Daniel 11.

_____

_____

_____

_____

For the Group

You may want to focus your discussion for lesson 11 especially on the following issues, themes, and concepts. (These will likely reflect what group members have learned in their individual study of this week's passage, although they'll also have made discoveries in other areas as well.)

• God's sovereignty over all things
• Perseverance
• Deliverance
• Eternal life
• Righteousness
• Wisdom and understanding
• The nature of evil
• Future history and the end of this world

The following numbered questions in lesson 11 may stimulate your best and most helpful discussion: 10, 11, 12, 14, 15, 16, and 17.

Remember to look also at the "For Thought and Discussion" questions in the margin.

1. Joyce G. Baldwin, *Daniel: An Introduction and Commentary*, vol. 25, Tyndale Old Testament Commentary (Downers Grove, IL: InterVarsity, 1978), 204.
2. Sinclair Ferguson, *Daniel*, The Preacher's Commentary, ed. Lloyd J. Ogilvie (Nashville: Thomas Nelson, 1988), 206.
3. Leland Ryken and Philip Graham Ryken, eds., *The Literary Study Bible* (Wheaton, IL: Crossway, 2007), at Daniel 11.
4. Baldwin, 203, 205.
5. Ferguson, 199.
6. *ESV Study Bible* (Wheaton, IL: Crossway, 2008), at Daniel 11:2-45.
7. Ferguson, 203.
8. Baldwin, 212–213.
9. Ferguson, 160–161.
10. Ferguson, 216.
11. Ferguson, 214–215.
12. *ESV*, at Daniel 11:33-35.
13. Baldwin, 217.
14. *Life Application Bible*, various editions (Wheaton, IL: Tyndale, 1988 and later), at Daniel 11:35.
15. *Life Application*, at Daniel 11:35.
16. Ferguson, 218–219.
17. *NIV Study Bible* (Grand Rapids, MI: Zondervan, 1985), at Daniel 11:36.
18. Ferguson, 219.
19. *Life Application*, at Daniel 11:45.
20. Ferguson, 221.
21. Ferguson, 222.

LESSON TWELVE

DANIEL 12

Looking to the End

This chapter brings to a conclusion the heavenly message for Daniel that was begun in chapter 10.

"At the end of the book the writer once again, as in chapters 2 and 7, takes us to the end of time."[1]

1. What is the importance of what Daniel further learns in verses 1 and 2 of this chapter?

   _____

   _____

   _____

   _____

2. What particular significance do you see in the information Daniel is given in verse 3?

   _____

   _____

   _____

   _____

For Further Study: What links do you see between the deliverance for God's people mentioned in Daniel 12:1 and the divine protection mentioned in Psalm 91:11-12?

For Further Study:
Regarding the topic of resurrection as brought up in Daniel 12:2, what links do you see in the words of Jesus in Matthew 25:46 and John 5:28-29?

Optional Application: What personal significance do you find for the promises stated in Daniel 12:3? Can you see yourself in this imagery?

Multitudes (12:2). These may represent "those who have been put to death in the great tribulation [described in 12:1]. . . . Not even the terrible time of suffering can destroy the certainty of the resurrection."[2]

Those who are wise (12:3). "The identity of 'the wise' is left open-ended. Despite many attempts that have been made to identify them with one and another group of Jewish society, the possibility remains that the author may have had in mind others besides Jews who would 'turn many to righteousness.'"[3]

3. Summarize the instructions Daniel is given in verse 4 and the reason for them.

_____

_____

_____

_____

"[Daniel 12:1-4] is the clearest Old Testament reference to the resurrection of the dead."[4]

Roll up and seal the words . . . until the time of the end (12:4). The scroll "was to be kept safe and preserved. This was to be done so that believers of all times could look back on God's work in history and find hope. Daniel did not understand the exact meaning of the times and events in his vision. We can see events as they unfold, for we are in the end times. The whole book will not be understood until the climax of earth's history."[5] "It must be on record for God's people so that the events of the end will not take them by surprise."[6]

Until the time of the end (12:4). "The implication of this passage is that the understanding of these visions would be made clear 'at the time of the end.'"[7]

To increase knowledge (12:4). This statement "is best understood as a further contrast between the lifestyle of the citizens of God's city and that of the citizens of the city of destruction—not only in the long term (verses 2-8) but also in the short term. While believers are able to rest secure in the knowledge of God they receive through God's Word, unbelievers are agitated in their search for the truth. . . . Apart from the knowledge of God's Word, that increased knowledge will simply be in vain."[8]

4. What else does Daniel go on to see and hear in verses 5-6?

_____

_____

_____

_____

How long will it be? (12:6). "It is the very question Daniel himself (and not only Daniel) would like to ask."[9]

5. What is the significance of the further message given to Daniel in verse 7?

_____

_____

_____

_____

A time, times and half a time (12:7). This phrase "conveys a sense of extended periods of time, but it also conveys something of God's

For Further Study: Tell how the quest for increased knowledge portrayed in the final sentence of Daniel 12:4 is also reflected in these passages: Amos 8:12; Romans 1:25; 2 Thessalonians 2:11.

For Thought and Discussion: Of all the things Daniel is told in this chapter, which phrases strike you most memorably and powerfully?

sovereign control over all events. By His own power He is able to cut short apparently inevitable historical developments."[10]

6. In verse 8, what is the importance of Daniel's response and his resulting question?

_____

_____

_____

_____

I did not understand. So I asked (12:8). "His great concern was to know when and how all this would come to an end. It was not for Daniel to know."[11]

7. What are the most important elements in the message given to Daniel in verses 9-12?

_____

_____

_____

_____

The time that the daily sacrifice is abolished and the abomination that causes desolation is set up (12:11). "That is, in the days of Antiochus Epiphanes [175–164 BC]."[12] See also Daniel 8:13; 9:27; 11:31.

1,290 days . . . 1,335 days (12:11-12). Each figure is just over three and a half years; the period is "measured in days, however, in order to underline that it has been carefully measured and is completely controlled by God. It will not last forever. . . . All this serves to emphasize that God alone changes the times and seasons (Daniel 2:21)."[13]

Blessed is the one who waits for and reaches the end (12:12). "Thus, as in the teaching of Jesus (Mark 13:13), the emphasis is on endurance to the end."[14]

8. What do you find most significant in the final instructions given to Daniel in verse 13?

_____

_____

_____

_____

"The Book of Daniel ends on a note of great promise which is often overlooked."[15]

Go your way (12:9,13). "He too must go on, though he is already an old man."[16]

9. What parallels do you see between what Daniel sees in this chapter and his vision in chapter 8?

_____

_____

_____

_____

10. From what Daniel sees and experiences in this chapter, what would you say he is learning most about God?

_____

_____

_____

_____

For Further Study: What links do you see between Daniel 12:13 and the New Testament exhortations in 2 Peter 3:11 and Matthew 25:21?

Optional Application: "Much of the meaning of Daniel's vision [in chapters 10–12] will become clear only when it is fulfilled. It is to be received by faith in such a way that we continue to live by faith, and not by sight."[17] What do you see as your own proper response of faith to the things you have studied in these final chapters of Daniel?

For Further Study:
"The principal passages and motifs from the Book of Daniel that are reflected or enlarged on in the New Testament largely relate to end-time events and personages."[18] In particular, the books of Daniel and Revelation have often been seen as closely linked. Reflect on what you have studied in Daniel and then describe what allusions to this book you can find in the following passages of Revelation: 1:14-15,17; 2:20; 4:2; 5:1,6,9,11; 9:20; 10:5-6; 11:3; 12:3-4; 13:1,5,11; 20:4,12.

11. In Daniel 12, what would you select as the key verse or passage—one that best captures or reflects the dynamics of what this chapter is all about?

_____

_____

_____

_____

12. List any lingering questions you have about Daniel 12.

_____

_____

_____

_____

Reviewing Daniel

13. Remember again God's reminder in Isaiah 55:10-11 — that in the same way He sends rain and snow from the sky to water the earth and nurture life, He sends His words to accomplish specific purposes. What would you suggest are God's primary purposes for the message of Daniel in the lives of His people today?

_____

_____

_____

14. The introduction to this study mentions the following as a universal question that is dealt with in Daniel: "How can followers of God maintain their loyalty to him while living in cultures that are hostile to biblical religion?"[19] How has your study of this book enabled you to better answer that question?

_____

_____

_____

15. The introduction also mentioned the following universal question as one dealt with in Daniel: "What does the future hold, and how will history end?"[20] Again, how has your study of this book enabled you to better answer that question?

_____

_____

_____

_____

Optional Application: Which verses in Daniel would be most helpful for you to memorize so you have them always available in your mind and heart for the Holy Spirit to use?

16. Recall once again the guidelines given for our thought-life in Philippians 4:8 — "Whatever is true, whatever is noble, whatever is right, whatever is pure, whatever is lovely, whatever is admirable — if anything is excellent or praiseworthy — *think about such things*" (emphasis added). As you reflect on all you've read in the book of Daniel, what stands out to you as being particularly *true*, or *noble*, or *right*, or *pure*, or *lovely*, or *admirable*, or *excellent*, or *praiseworthy* — and therefore well worth thinking more about?

_____

_____

_____

_____

17. Because all of Scripture testifies ultimately of Christ, where does *Jesus* come most in focus for you in this book?

_____

_____

_____

18. In your understanding, what are the strongest ways Daniel points us to mankind's need for Jesus and what He accomplished in His death and resurrection?

_____

_____

_____

_____

19. Recall again Paul's reminder that the Old Testament Scriptures can give us patience and perseverance on one hand as well as comfort and encouragement on the other (see Romans 15:4). In your own life, how do you see the book of Daniel living up to Paul's description? In what ways does it help to meet your personal needs for both *perseverance* and *encouragement*?

_____

_____

_____

_____

For the Group

You may want to focus your discussion for lesson 12 especially on the following issues, themes, and concepts. (These will likely reflect what group members have learned in their individual study of this week's passage, although they'll also have made discoveries in other areas as well.)

- God's sovereignty over all things
- True heroism
- Godliness
- Future history and the end of this world

The following numbered questions in lesson 12 may stimulate your best and most helpful discussion: 1, 2, 8, 10, 11, and 12.

Allow enough discussion time to look back together and review all of Daniel as a whole. You can use the numbered questions 13–19 in this lesson to help you do that.

Look also at the questions in the margin under the heading "For Thought and Discussion."

1. Joyce G. Baldwin, *Daniel: An Introduction and Commentary*, vol. 25, Tyndale Old Testament Commentary (Downers Grove, IL: InterVarsity, 1978), 69.
2. Sinclair Ferguson, *Daniel*, The Preacher's Commentary, ed. Lloyd J. Ogilvie (Nashville: Thomas Nelson, 1988), 226.
3. Baldwin, 59.
4. *The Complete Word Study Old Testament*, ed. Warren Baker (Chattanooga, TN: AMG Publishers, 1994), at Daniel 12:1-4.
5. *Life Application Bible*, various editions (Wheaton, IL: Tyndale, 1988 and later), at Daniel 12:4.
6. Ferguson, 227.
7. *Complete Word Study*, at Daniel 12:1-4.
8. Ferguson, 227.
9. Ferguson, 229.
10. Ferguson, 229.
11. Ferguson, 229.
12. Ferguson, 230.
13. Ferguson, 230.
14. Baldwin, 232.
15. *Complete Word Study*, at Daniel 12:13.
16. Baldwin, 232.
17. Ferguson, 230.
18. Gleason L. Archer Jr., *Daniel*, vol. 7, Expositor's Bible Commentary, ed. Frank E. Gaebelein (Grand Rapids, MI: Zondervan, 1985), 12.
19. Leland Ryken and Philip Graham Ryken, eds., *The Literary Study Bible* (Wheaton, IL: Crossway, 2007), intro to Daniel, "The book at a glance."
20. Ryken and Ryken, intro to Daniel, "The book at a glance."

STUDY AIDS

For further information on the material in this study, consider the following sources. They are available on the Internet (www.christianbook.com, www.amazon.com, and so on), or your local Christian bookstore should be able to order any of them if it does not carry them. Most seminary libraries have them, as well as many university and public libraries. If they are out of print, you may be able to find them online.

Commentaries on Daniel

Gleason L. Archer Jr., *Daniel*, vol. 7, Expositor's Bible Commentary, ed. Frank E. Gaebelein (Grand Rapids, MI: Zondervan, 1985).

Joyce G. Baldwin, *Daniel: An Introduction and Commentary*, vol. 25, Tyndale Old Testament Commentary (Downers Grove, IL: InterVarsity, 1978).

James Montgomery Boice, *Daniel* (Grand Rapids, MI: Baker, 2006).

Sinclair Ferguson, *Daniel*, The Preacher's Commentary, ed. Lloyd J. Ogilvie (Nashville: Thomas Nelson, 1988).

John Calvin, *Commentaries on the Book of the Prophet Daniel*, 2 vols., trans. Thomas Myers (Grand Rapids, MI: Eerdmans, 1948).

Bryan Chapell, *Standing Your Ground: A Call to Courage in an Age of Compromise: Messages from Daniel* (Grand Rapids, MI: Baker, 1989).

John Joseph Collins, *Daniel: A Commentary on the Book of Daniel*, Hermeneia series (Minneapolis: Fortress, 1993).

Iain M. Duguid, *Daniel*, Reformed Expository Commentary series (Phillipsburg, NJ: P&R, 2008).

John E. Goldingay, *Daniel*, vol. 30, Word Biblical Commentary (Dallas: Word, 1989).

Tremper Longman III, *Daniel*, The NIV Application Commentary series (Grand Rapids, MI: Zondervan, 1999).

Ernest Lucas, *Daniel*, Apollos Old Testament Commentary series (Downers Grove, IL: InterVarsity, 2002).

Ronald S. Wallace, *The Message of Daniel: The Lord is King*, The Bible Speaks Today series (Downers Grove, IL: InterVarsity, 1984).

Edward J. Young, *The Prophecy of Daniel: Introduction and Commentary* (Grand Rapids, MI: Eerdmans, 1977).

Historical Background Sources and Handbooks

Bible study becomes more meaningful when modern Western readers understand the times and places in which the biblical authors lived. *The IVP Bible Background Commentary: Old Testament*, by John H. Walton, Victor H. Matthews, and Mark Chavalas (InterVarsity, 2000), provides insight into the ancient Near Eastern world, its peoples, customs, and geography to help contemporary readers better understand the context in which the Old Testament Scriptures were written.

A **handbook** of biblical customs can also be useful. Some good ones are the time-proven updated classic *Halley's Bible Handbook with the New International Version*, by Henry H. Halley (Zondervan, 2007), and the inexpensive paperback *Manners and Customs in the Bible*, by Victor H. Matthews (Hendrickson, 1991).

Concordances, Dictionaries, and Encyclopedias

A **concordance** lists words of the Bible alphabetically along with each verse in which the word appears. It lets you do your own word studies. An *exhaustive* concordance lists every word used in a given translation, while an *abridged* or *complete* concordance omits either some words, some occurrences of the word, or both.

Two of the best exhaustive concordances are *Strong's Exhaustive Concordance* and *The Strongest NIV Exhaustive Concordance*. *Strong's* is available based on the KJV and NASB. *Strong's* has an index by which you can find out which Greek or Hebrew word is used in a given English verse. The NIV concordance does the same thing except it also includes an index for Aramaic words in the original texts from which the NIV was translated. However, neither concordance requires knowledge of the original languages. *Strong's* is available online at www.biblestudytools.com. Both are also available in hard copy.

A **Bible dictionary** or **Bible encyclopedia** alphabetically lists articles about people, places, doctrines, important words, customs, and geography of the Bible.

Holman Illustrated Bible Dictionary, edited by C. Brand, C. W. Draper, and A. England (B&H, 2003), offers more than seven hundred color photos, illustrations, and charts; sixty full-color maps; and up-to-date archeological findings, along with exhaustive definitions of people, places, things, and events—dealing with every subject in the Bible. It uses a variety of Bible translations and is the only dictionary that includes the HCSB, NIV, KJV, RSV, NRSV, REB, NASB, ESV, and TEV.

The New Unger's Bible Dictionary, Revised and Expanded, by Merrill

F. Unger (Moody, 2006), has been a best seller for more than fifty years. Its 6,700-plus entries reflect the most current scholarship and more than 1,200,000 words are supplemented with detailed essays, colorful photography and maps, and dozens of charts and illustrations to enhance your understanding of God's Word. Based on the NASB.

The Zondervan Encyclopedia of the Bible, edited by Moisés Silva and Merrill C. Tenney (Zondervan, 2008), is excellent and exhaustive. However, its five 1,000-page volumes are a financial investment, so all but very serious students may prefer to use it at a church, public, college, or seminary library.

Unlike a Bible dictionary in the above sense, *Vine's Complete Expository Dictionary of Old and New Testament Words,* by W. E. Vine, Merrill F. Unger, and William White Jr. (Thomas Nelson, 1996), alphabetically lists major words used in the KJV and defines each Old Testament Hebrew or New Testament Greek word the KJV translates with that English word. *Vine's* lists verse references where that Hebrew or Greek word appears so that you can do your own cross-references and word studies without knowing the original languages.

The Brown-Driver-Briggs Hebrew and English Lexicon by Francis Brown, C. Briggs, and S. R. Driver (Hendrickson, 1996), is probably the most respected and comprehensive Bible lexicon for Old Testament studies. *BDB* gives not only dictionary definitions for each word but relates each word to its Old Testament usage and categorizes its nuances of meaning.

Bible Atlases and Map Books

A **Bible atlas** can be a great aid to understanding what is going on in a book of the Bible and how geography affected events. Here are a few good choices:

The Hammond Atlas of Bible Lands (Langenscheidt, 2007) packs a ton of resources into just sixty-four pages. Maps, of course, but also photographs, illustrations, and a comprehensive timeline. It includes an introduction to the unique geography of the Holy Land, including terrain, trade routes, vegetation, and climate information.

The New Moody Atlas of the Bible, by Barry J. Beitzel (Moody, 2009), is scholarly, very evangelical, and full of theological text, indexes, and references. Beitzel shows vividly how God prepared the land of Israel perfectly for the acts of salvation He was going to accomplish in it.

Then and Now Bible Maps Insert (Rose, 2008) is a nifty paperback that is sized just right to fit inside your Bible cover. Only forty-four pages long, it features clear plastic overlays of modern-day cities and countries so you can see what nation or city now occupies the Bible setting you are reading about. Every major city of the Bible is included.

For Small-Group Leaders

Discipleship Journal's Best Small-Group Ideas, Vols. 1 and 2 (NavPress, 2005). Each volume is packed with 101 of the best hands-on tips and group-building principles from *Discipleship Journal*'s "Small Group Letter" and "DJ Plus" as well as articles from the magazine. They will help you inject new passion into the life of your small group.

Donahue, Bill. *Leading Life-Changing Small Groups* (Zondervan, 2002). This comprehensive resource is packed with information, practical tips, and insights that will teach you about small-group philosophy and structure, discipleship, conducting meetings, and more.

McBride, Neal F. *How to Lead Small Groups* (NavPress, 1990). This book covers leadership skills for all kinds of small groups: Bible study, fellowship, task, and support groups. It's filled with step-by-step guidance and practical exercises to help you grasp the critical aspects of small-group leadership and dynamics.

Miller, Tara, and Jenn Peppers. *Finding the Flow: A Guide for Leading Small Groups and Gatherings* (IVP Connect, 2008). *Finding the Flow* offers a fresh take on leading small groups by seeking to develop the leader's small-group facilitation skills.

Bible Study Methods

Discipleship Journal's Best Bible Study Methods (NavPress, 2002). This is a collection of thirty-two creative ways to explore Scripture that will help you enjoy studying God's Word more.

Hendricks, Howard, and William Hendricks. *Living by the Book: The Art and Science of Reading the Bible* (Moody, 2007). *Living by the Book* offers a practical three-step process that will help you master simple yet effective inductive methods of observation, interpretation, and application that will make all the difference in your time with God's Word. A workbook by the same title is also available to go along with the book.

The Navigator Bible Studies Handbook (NavPress, 1994). This resource teaches the underlying principles for doing good inductive Bible study, including instructions on doing question-and-answer studies, verse-analysis studies, chapter-analysis studies, and topical studies.

Warren, Rick. *Rick Warren's Bible Study Methods: Twelve Ways You Can Unlock God's Word* (HarperCollins, 2006). Rick Warren offers simple, step-by-step instructions, guiding you through twelve different approaches to studying the Bible for yourself with the goal of becoming more like Jesus.

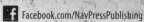 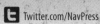